# The Witch Of Atlas & Other Longer Poems by Percy Bysshe Shelley

Percy Bysshe Shelley is one of the most revered figures in the English poetical landscape. Born on the 4th August 1792 he has, over the years, become rightly regarded as a major Romantic poet. Yet during his own lifetime little of his work was published. Publishers feared his radical views and possible charges against themselves for blasphemy and sedition. On 8th July 1822 a month before his 30th birthday, during a sudden storm, his tragic early death by drowning robbed our culture of many fine expected masterpieces. But in his short spell on earth he weaved much magic. Among his many great works is The Witch Of Atlas which is published here along with several other classics. Shelley's words are alive with intent, meaning and emotion. A true poet for all our ages.

## Index Of Contents
The Witch Of Atlas
Epipsychidion
Julian And Maddalo. A Conversation.
Preface
Julian And Maddalo
Alastor: Or, The Spirit Of Solitude - Preface
Alastor: Or, The Spirit Of Solitude

## THE WITCH OF ATLAS

**To Mary (On Her Objecting to the Following Poem, Upon the Score of its Containing No Human Interest)**

I.
How, my dear Mary, are you critic-bitten
(For vipers kill, though dead) by some review,
That you condemn these verses I have written,
Because they tell no story, false or true?
What, though no mice are caught by a young kitten,
May it not leap and play as grown cats do,
Till its claws come? Prithee, for this one time,
Content thee with a visionary rhyme.

II.
What hand would crush the silken-wingèd fly,
The youngest of inconstant April's minions,
Because it cannot climb the purest sky,
Where the swan sings, amid the sun's dominions?
Not thine. Thou knowest 'tis its doom to die,
When Day shall hide within her twilight pinions

The lucent eyes, and the eternal smile,
Serene as thine, which lent it life awhile.

III.
To thy fair feet a wingèd Vision came,
Whose date should have been longer than a day,
And o'er thy head did beat its wings for fame,
And in thy sight its fading plumes display;
The watery bow burned in the evening flame,
But the shower fell, the swift Sun went his way
And that is dead. O, let me not believe
That anything of mine is fit to live!

IV.
Wordsworth informs us he was nineteen years
Considering and retouching Peter Bell;
Watering his laurels with the killing tears
Of slow, dull care, so that their roots to Hell
Might pierce, and their wide branches blot the spheres
Of Heaven, with dewy leaves and flowers; this well
May be, for Heaven and Earth conspire to foil
The over-busy gardener's blundering toil.

V.
My Witch indeed is not so sweet a creature
As Ruth or Lucy, whom his graceful praise
Clothes for our grandsons but she matches Peter,
Though he took nineteen years, and she three days
In dressing. Light the vest of flowing metre
She wears; he, proud as dandy with his stays,
Has hung upon his wiry limbs a dress
Like King Lear's "looped and windowed raggedness."

VI.
If you strip Peter, you will see a fellow
Scorched by Hell's hyperequatorial climate
Into a kind of a sulphureous yellow:
A lean mark, hardly fit to fling a rhyme at;
In shape a Scaramouch, in hue Othello.
If you unveil my Witch, no priest nor primate
Can shrive you of that sin, f sin there be
In love, when it becomes idolatry.


The Witch of Atlas

I.

Before those cruel Twins, whom at one birth
Incestuous Change bore to her father Time,
Error and Truth, had hunted from the Earth
All those bright natures which adorned its prime,
And left us nothing to believe in, worth
The pains of putting into learnèd rhyme,
A lady-witch there lived on Atlas' mountain
Within a cavern, by a secret fountain.

II.
Her mother was one of the Atlantides:
The all-beholding Sun had ne'er beholden
In his wide voyage o'er continents and seas
So fair a creature, as she lay enfolden
In the warm shadow of her loveliness;
He kissed her with his beams, and made all golden
The chamber of gray rock in which she lay
She, in that dream of joy, dissolved away.

III.
'Tis said, she first was changed into a vapour,
And then into a cloud, such clouds as flit,
Like splendour-wingèd moths about a taper,
Round the red west when the sun dies in it:
And then into a meteor, such as caper
On hill-tops when the moon is in a fit:
Then, into one of those mysterious stars
Which hide themselves between the Earth and Mars.

IV.
Ten times the Mother of the Months had bent
Her bow beside the folding-star, and bidden
With that bright sign the billows to indent
The sea-deserted sand like children chidden,
At her command they ever came and went
Since in that cave a dewy splendour hidden
Took shape and motion: with the living form
Of this embodied Power, the cave grew warm.

V.
A lovely lady garmented in light
From her own beauty, deep her eyes, as are
Two openings of unfathomable night
Seen through a Temple's cloven roof, her hair
Dark, the dim brain whirls dizzy with delight,
Picturing her form; her soft smiles shone afar,
And her low voice was heard like love, and drew

All living things towards this wonder new.

VI.
And first the spotted cameleopard came,
And then the wise and fearless elephant;
Then the sly serpent, in the golden flame
Of his own volumes intervolved; all gaunt
And sanguine beasts her gentle looks made tame.
They drank before her at her sacred fount;
And every beast of beating heart grew bold,
Such gentleness and power even to behold.

VII.
The brinded lioness led forth her young,
That she might teach them how they should forego
Their inborn thirst of death; the pard unstrung
His sinews at her feet, and sought to know
With looks whose motions spoke without a tongue
How he might be as gentle as the doe.
The magic circle of her voice and eyes
All savage natures did imparadise.

VIII.
And old Silenus, shaking a green stick
Of lilies, and the wood-gods in a crew
Came, blithe, as in the olive copses thick
Cicadae are, drunk with the noonday dew:
And Dryope and Faunus followed quick,
Teasing the God to sing them something new;
Till in this cave they found the lady lone,
Sitting upon a seat of emerald stone.

IX.
And universal Pan, 'tis said, was there,
And though none saw him, through the adamant
Of the deep mountains, through the trackless air,
And through those living spirits, like a want,
He passed out of his everlasting lair
Where the quick heart of the great world doth pant,
And felt that wondrous lady all alone,
And she felt him, upon her emerald throne.

X.
And every nymph of stream and spreading tree,
And every shepherdess of Ocean's flocks,
Who drives her white waves over the green sea,
And Ocean with the brine on his gray locks,

And quaint Priapus with his company,
All came, much wondering how the enwombèd rocks
Could have brought forth so beautiful a birth; v
Her love subdued their wonder and their mirth.

XI.
The herdsmen and the mountain maidens came,
And the rude kings of pastoral Garamant
Their spirits shook within them, as a flame
Stirred by the air under a cavern gaunt:
Pigmies, and Polyphemes, by many a name,
Centaurs, and Satyrs, and such shapes as haunt
Wet clefts, and lumps neither alive nor dead,
Dog-headed, bosom-eyed, and bird-footed.

XII.
For she was beautiful, her beauty made
The bright world dim, and everything beside
Seemed like the fleeting image of a shade:
No thought of living spirit could abide,
Which to her looks had ever been betrayed,
On any object in the world so wide,
On any hope within the circling skies,
But on her form, and in her inmost eyes.

XIII.
Which when the lady knew, she took her spindle
And twined three threads of fleecy mist, and three
Long lines of light, such as the dawn may kindle
The clouds and waves and mountains with; and she
As many star-beams, ere their lamps could dwindle
In the belated moon, wound skilfully;
And with these threads a subtle veil she wove
A shadow for the splendour of her love.

XIV.
The deep recesses of her odorous dwelling
Were stored with magic treasures, sounds of air,
Which had the power all spirits of compelling,
Folded in cells of crystal silence there;
Such as we hear in youth, and think the feeling
Will never die, yet ere we are aware,
The feeling and the sound are fled and gone,
And the regret they leave remains alone.

XV.
And there lay Visions swift, and sweet, and quaint,

Each in its thin sheath, like a chrysalis,
Some eager to burst forth, some weak and faint
With the soft burthen of intensest bliss
It was its work to bear to many a saint
Whose heart adores the shrine which holiest is,
Even Love's: and others white, green, gray, and black,
And of all shapes and each was at her beck.

XVI.
And odours in a kind of aviary
Of ever-blooming Eden-trees she kept,
Clipped in a floating net, a love-sick Fairy
Had woven from dew-beams while the moon yet slept;
As bats at the wired window of a dairy.
They beat their vans; and each was an adept,
When loosed and missioned, making wings of winds,
To stir sweet thoughts or sad, in destined minds.

XVII.
And liquors clear and sweet, whose healthful might
Could medicine the sick soul to happy sleep,
And change eternal death into a night
Of glorious dreams or if eyes needs must weep,
Could make their tears all wonder and delight,
She in her crystal vials did closely keep:
If men could drink of those clear vials, 'tis said
The living were not envied of the dead.

XVIII.
Her cave was stored with scrolls of strange device,
The works of some Saturnian Archimage,
Which taught the expiations at whose price
Men from the Gods might win that happy age
Too lightly lost, redeeming native vice;
And which might quench the Earth-consuming rage
Of gold and blood till men should live and move
Harmonious as the sacred stars above;

XIX.
And how all things that seem untameable,
Not to be checked and not to be confined,
Obey the spells of Wisdom's wizard skill;
Time, earth, and fire, the ocean and the wind,
And all their shapes and man's imperial will;
And other scrolls whose writings did unbind
The inmost lore of Love, let the profane
Tremble to ask what secrets they contain.

XX.
And wondrous works of substances unknown,
To which the enchantment of her father's power
Had changed those ragged blocks of savage stone,
Were heaped in the recesses of her bower;
Carved lamps and chalices, and vials which shone
In their own golden beams, each like a flower,
Out of whose depth a fire-fly shakes his light
Under a cypress in a starless night.

XXI.
At first she lived alone in this wild home,
And her own thoughts were each a minister,
Clothing themselves, or with the ocean foam,
Or with the wind, or with the speed of fire,
To work whatever purposes might come
Into her mind; such power her mighty Sire
Had girt them with, whether to fly or run,
Through all the regions which he shines upon.

XXII.
The Ocean-nymphs and Hamadryades,
Oreads and Naiads, with long weedy locks,
Offered to do her bidding through the seas,
Under the earth, and in the hollow rocks,
And far beneath the matted roots of trees,
And in the gnarlèd heart of stubborn oaks,
So they might live for ever in the light
Of her sweet presence,  each a satellite.

XXIII.
"This may not be," the wizard maid replied;
"The fountains where the Naiades bedew
Their shining hair, at length are drained and dried;
The solid oaks forget their strength, and strew
Their latest leaf upon the mountains wide;
The boundless ocean like a drop of dew
Will be consumed, the stubborn centre must
Be scattered, like a cloud of summer dust.

XXIV.
"And ye with them will perish, one by one;
If I must sigh to think that this shall be,
If I must weep when the surviving Sun
Shall smile on your decay, oh, ask not me
To love you till your little race is run;

I cannot die as ye must over me
Your leaves shall glance, the streams in which ye dwell
Shall be my paths henceforth, and so farewell!"

XXV.
She spoke and wept: the dark and azure well
Sparkled beneath the shower of her bright tears,
And every little circlet where they fell
Flung to the cavern-roof inconstant spheres
And intertangled lines of light: a knell
Of sobbing voices came upon her ears
From those departing Forms, o'er the serene
Of the white streams and of the forest green.

XXVI.
All day the wizard lady sate aloof,
Spelling out scrolls of dread antiquity,
Under the cavern's fountain-lighted roof;
Or broidering the pictured poesy
Of some high tale upon her growing woof,
Which the sweet splendour of her smiles could dye
In hues outshining heaven and ever she
Added some grace to the wrought poesy.

XXVII.
While on her hearth lay blazing many a piece
Of sandal wood, rare gums, and cinnamon;
Men scarcely know how beautiful fire is
Each flame of it is as a precious stone
Dissolved in ever-moving light, and this
Belongs to each and all who gaze upon.
The Witch beheld it not, for in her hand
She held a woof that dimmed the burning brand.

XXVIII.
This lady never slept, but lay in trance
All night within the fountain as in sleep.
Its emerald crags glowed in her beauty's glance;
Through the green splendour of the water deep
She saw the constellations reel and dance
Like fire-flies and withal did ever keep
The tenour of her contemplations calm,
With open eyes, closed feet, and folded palm.

XXIX.
And when the whirlwinds and the clouds descended
From the white pinnacles of that cold hill,

She passed at dewfall to a space extended,
Where in a lawn of flowering asphodel
Amid a wood of pines and cedars blended,
There yawned an inextinguishable well
Of crimson fire, full even to the brim,
And overflowing all the margin trim.

XXX.
Within the which she lay when the fierce war
Of wintry winds shook that innocuous liquor
In many a mimic moon and bearded star
O'er woods and lawns; the serpent heard it flicker
In sleep, and dreaming still, he crept afar
And when the windless snow descended thicker
Than autumn leaves, she watched it as it came
Melt on the surface of the level flame.

XXXI.
She had a boat, which some say Vulcan wrought
For Venus, as the chariot of her star;
But it was found too feeble to be fraught
With all the ardours in that sphere which are,
And so she sold it, and Apollo bought
And gave it to this daughter: from a car
Changed to the fairest and the lightest boat
Which ever upon mortal stream did float.

XXXII.
And others say, that, when but three hours old,
The first-born Love out of his cradle lept,
And clove dun Chaos with his wings of gold,
And like an horticultural adept,
Stole a strange seed, and wrapped it up in mould,
And sowed it in his mother's star, and kept
Watering it all the summer with sweet dew,
And with his wings fanning it as it grew.

XXXIII.
The plant grew strong and green, the snowy flower
Fell, and the long and gourd-like fruit began
To turn the light and dew by inward power
To its own substance; woven tracery ran
Of light firm texture, ribbed and branching, o'er
The solid rind, like a leaf's veinèd fan
Of which Love scooped this boat and with soft motion
Piloted it round the circumfluous ocean.

XXXIV.
This boat she moored upon her fount, and lit
A living spirit within all its frame,
Breathing the soul of swiftness into it.
Couched on the fountain like a panther tame,
One of the twain at Evan's feet that sit
Or as on Vesta's sceptre a swift flame
Or on blind Homer's heart a wingèd thought,
In joyous expectation lay the boat.

XXXV.
Then by strange art she kneaded fire and snow
Together, tempering the repugnant mass
With liquid love, all things together grow
Through which the harmony of love can pass;
And a fair Shape out of her hands did flow
A living Image, which did far surpass
In beauty that bright shape of vital stone
Which drew the heart out of Pygmalion.

XXXVI.
A sexless thing it was, and in its growth
It seemed to have developed no defect
Of either sex, yet all the grace of both,
In gentleness and strength its limbs were decked;
The bosom swelled lightly with its full youth,
The countenance was such as might select
Some artist that his skill should never die,
Imaging forth such perfect purity.

XXXVII.
From its smooth shoulders hung two rapid wings,
Fit to have borne it to the seventh sphere,
Tipped with the speed of liquid lightenings,
Dyed in the ardours of the atmosphere:
She led her creature to the boiling springs
Where the light boat was moored, and said: "Sit here!"
And pointed to the prow, and took her seat
Beside the rudder, with opposing feet.

XXXVIII.
And down the streams which clove those mountains vast,
Around their inland islets, and amid
The panther-peopled forests, whose shade cast
Darkness and odours, and a pleasure hid
In melancholy gloom, the pinnace passed;
By many a star-surrounded pyramid

Of icy crag cleaving the purple sky,
And caverns yawning round unfathomably.

XXXIX.
The silver noon into that winding dell,
With slanted gleam athwart the forest tops,
Tempered like golden evening, feebly fell;
A green and glowing light, like that which drops
From folded lilies in which glow-worms dwell,
When Earth over her face Night's mantle wraps;
Between the severed mountains lay on high,
Over the stream, a narrow rift of sky.

XL.
And ever as she went, the Image lay
With folded wings and unawakened eyes;
And o'er its gentle countenance did play
The busy dreams, as thick as summer flies,
Chasing the rapid smiles that would not stay,
And drinking the warm tears, and the sweet sighs
Inhaling, which, with busy murmur vain,
They had aroused from that full heart and brain.

XLI.
And ever down the prone vale, like a cloud
Upon a stream of wind, the pinnace went:
Now lingering on the pools, in which abode
The calm and darkness of the deep content
In which they paused; now o'er the shallow road
Of white and dancing waters, all besprent
With sand and polished pebbles: mortal boat
In such a shallow rapid could not float.

XLII.
And down the earthquaking cataracts which shiver
Their snow-like waters into golden air,
Or under chasms unfathomable ever
Sepulchre them, till in their rage they tear
A subterranean portal for the river,
It fled, the circling sunbows did upbear
Its fall down the hoar precipice of spray,
Lighting it far upon its lampless way.

XLIII.
And when the wizard lady would ascend
The labyrinths of some many-winding vale,
Which to the inmost mountain upward tend

She called "Hermaphroditus!" and the pale
And heavy hue which slumber could extend
Over its lips and eyes, as on the gale
A rapid shadow from a slope of grass,
Into the darkness of the stream did pass.

XLIV.
And it unfurled its heaven-coloured pinions,
With stars of fire spotting the stream below;
And from above into the Sun's dominions
Flinging a glory, like the golden glow
In which Spring clothes her emerald-wingèd minions,
All interwoven with fine feathery snow
And moonlight splendour of intensest rime,
With which frost paints the pines in winter time.

XLV.
And then it winnowed the Elysian air
Whichever hung about that lady bright,
With its aetherial vans and speeding there,
Like a star up the torrent of the night,
Or a swift eagle in the morning glare
Breasting the whirlwind with impetuous flight,
The pinnace, oared by those enchanted wings,
Clove the fierce streams towards their upper springs.

XLVI.
The water flashed, like sunlight by the prow
Of a noon-wandering meteor flung to Heaven;
The still air seemed as if its waves did flow
In tempest down the mountains; loosely driven
The lady's radiant hair streamed to and fro:
Beneath, the billows having vainly striven
Indignant and impetuous, roared to feel
The swift and steady motion of the keel.

XLVII.
Or, when the weary moon was in the wane,
Or in the noon of interlunar night,
The lady-witch in visions could not chain
Her spirit; but sailed forth under the light
Of shooting stars, and bade extend amain
Its storm-outspeeding wings, the Hermaphrodite;
She to the Austral waters took her way,
Beyond the fabulous Thamondocana,

XLVIII.

Where, like a meadow which no scythe has shaven,
Which rain could never bend, or whirl-blast shake,
With the Antarctic constellations paven,
Canopus and his crew, lay the Austral lake
There she would build herself a windless haven
Out of the clouds whose moving turrets make
The bastions of the storm, when through the sky
The spirits of the tempest thundered by:

XLIX.
A haven beneath whose translucent floor
The tremulous stars sparkled unfathomably,
And around which the solid vapours hoar,
Based on the level waters, to the sky
Lifted their dreadful crags, and like a shore
Of wintry mountains, inaccessibly
Hemmed in with rifts and precipices gray,
And hanging crags, many a cove and bay.

L.
And whilst the outer lake beneath the lash
Of the wind's scourge, foamed like a wounded thing,
And the incessant hail with stony clash
Ploughed up the waters, and the flagging wing
Of the roused cormorant in the lightning flash
Looked like the wreck of some wind-wandering
Fragment of inky thunder-smoke, this haven
Was as a gem to copy Heaven engraven,

LI.
On which that lady played her many pranks,
Circling the image of a shooting star,
Even as a tiger on Hydaspes' banks
Outspeeds the antelopes which speediest are,
In her light boat; and many quips and cranks
She played upon the water, till the car
Of the late moon, like a sick matron wan,
To journey from the misty east began.

LII.
And then she called out of the hollow turrets
Of those high clouds, white, golden and vermilion,
The armies of her ministering spirits
In mighty legions, million after million,
They came, each troop emblazoning its merits
On meteor flags; and many a proud pavilion
Of the intertexture of the atmosphere

They pitched upon the plain of the calm mere.

LIII.
They framed the imperial tent of their great Queen
Of woven exhalations, underlaid
With lambent lightning-fire, as may be seen
A dome of thin and open ivory inlaid
With crimson silk, cressets from the serene
Hung there, and on the water for her tread
A tapestry of fleece-like mist was strewn,
Dyed in the beams of the ascending moon.

LIV.
And on a throne o'erlaid with starlight, caught
Upon those wandering isles of aëry dew,
Which highest shoals of mountain shipwreck not,
She sate, and heard all that had happened new
Between the earth and moon, since they had brought
The last intelligence and now she grew
Pale as that moon, lost in the watery night
And now she wept, and now she laughed outright.

LV.
These were tame pleasures; she would often climb
The steepest ladder of the crudded rack
Up to some beakèd cape of cloud sublime,
And like Arion on the dolphin's back
Ride singing through the shoreless air; oft-time
Following the serpent lightning's winding track,
She ran upon the platforms of the wind,
And laughed to hear the fire-balls roar behind.

LVI.
And sometimes to those streams of upper air
Which whirl the earth in its diurnal round,
She would ascend, and win the spirits there
To let her join their chorus. Mortals found
That on those days the sky was calm and fair,
And mystic snatches of harmonious sound
Wandered upon the earth where'er she passed,
And happy thoughts of hope, too sweet to last.

LVII.
But her choice sport was, in the hours of sleep,
To glide adown old Nilus, where he threads
Egypt and AEthiopia, from the steep
Of utmost Axumè, until he spreads,

Like a calm flock of silver-fleecèd sheep,
His waters on the plain: and crested heads
Of cities and proud temples gleam amid,
And many a vapour-belted pyramid.

LVIII.
By Moeris and the Mareotid lakes,
Strewn with faint blooms like bridal chamber floors,
Where naked boys bridling tame water-snakes,
Or charioteering ghastly alligators,
Had left on the sweet waters mighty wakes
Of those huge forms, within the brazen doors
Of the great Labyrinth slept both boy and beast,
Tired with the pomp of their Osirian feast.

LIX.
And where within the surface of the river
The shadows of the massy temples lie,
And never are erased but tremble ever
Like things which every cloud can doom to die,
Through lotus-paven canals, and wheresoever
The works of man pierced that serenest sky
With tombs, and towers, and fanes, 'twas her delight
To wander in the shadow of the night.

LX.
With motion like the spirit of that wind
Whose soft step deepens slumber, her light feet
Passed through the peopled haunts of humankind,
Scattering sweet visions from her presence sweet,
Through fane, and palace-court, and labyrinth mined
With many a dark and subterranean street
Under the Nile, through chambers high and deep
She passed, observing mortals in their sleep.

LXI.
A pleasure sweet doubtless it was to see
Mortals subdued in all the shapes of sleep.
Here lay two sister twins in infancy;
There, a lone youth who in his dreams did weep;
Within, two lovers linked innocently
In their loose locks which over both did creep
Like ivy from one stem; and there lay calm
Old age with snow-bright hair and folded palm.

LXII.
But other troubled forms of sleep she saw,

Not to be mirrored in a holy song
Distortions foul of supernatural awe,
And pale imaginings of visioned wrong;
And all the code of Custom's lawless law
Written upon the brows of old and young:
"This," said the wizard maiden, "is the strife
Which stirs the liquid surface of man's life."

LXIII.
And little did the sight disturb her soul.
We, the weak mariners of that wide lake
Where'er its shores extend or billows roll,
Our course unpiloted and starless make
O'er its wild surface to an unknown goal:
But she in the calm depths her way could take,
Where in bright bowers immortal forms abide
Beneath the weltering of the restless tide.

LXIV.
And she saw princes couched under the glow
Of sunlike gems; and round each temple-court
In dormitories ranged, row after row,
She saw the priests asleep all of one sort
For all were educated to be so.
The peasants in their huts, and in the port
The sailors she saw cradled on the waves,
And the dead lulled within their dreamless graves.

LXV.
And all the forms in which those spirits lay
Were to her sight like the diaphanous
Veils, in which those sweet ladies oft array
Their delicate limbs, who would conceal from us
Only their scorn of all concealment: they
Move in the light of their own beauty thus.
But these and all now lay with sleep upon them,
And little thought a Witch was looking on them.

LXVI.
She, all those human figures breathing there,
Beheld as living spirits to her eyes
The naked beauty of the soul lay bare,
And often through a rude and worn disguise
She saw the inner form most bright and fair
And then she had a charm of strange device,
Which, murmured on mute lips with tender tone,
Could make that spirit mingle with her own.

LXVII.
Alas! Aurora, what wouldst thou have given
For such a charm when Tithon became gray?
Or how much, Venus, of thy silver heaven
Wouldst thou have yielded, ere Proserpina
Had half (oh! why not all?) the debt forgiven
Which dear Adonis had been doomed to pay,
To any witch who would have taught you it?
The Heliad doth not know its value yet.

LXVIII.
'Tis said in after times her spirit free
Knew what love was, and felt itself alone
But holy Dian could not chaster be
Before she stooped to kiss Endymion,
Than now this lady, like a sexless bee
Tasting all blossoms, and confined to none,
Among those mortal forms, the wizard-maiden
Passed with an eye serene and heart unladen.

LXIX.
To those she saw most beautiful, she gave
Strange panacea in a crystal bowl:
They drank in their deep sleep of that sweet wave,
And lived thenceforward as if some control,
Mightier than life, were in them; and the grave
Of such, when death oppressed the weary soul,
Was as a green and overarching bower
Lit by the gems of many a starry flower.

LXX.
For on the night when they were buried, she
Restored the embalmers' ruining, and shook
The light out of the funeral lamps, to be
A mimic day within that deathly nook;
And she unwound the woven imagery
Of second childhood's swaddling bands, and took
The coffin, its last cradle, from its niche,
And threw it with contempt into a ditch.

LXXI.
And there the body lay, age after age,
Mute, breathing, beating, warm, and undecaying,
Like one asleep in a green hermitage,
With gentle smiles about its eyelids playing,
And living in its dreams beyond the rage

Of death or life; while they were still arraying
In liveries ever new, the rapid, blind
And fleeting generations of mankind.

LXXII.
And she would write strange dreams upon the brain
Of those who were less beautiful, and make
All harsh and crooked purposes more vain
Than in the desert is the serpent's wake
Which the sand covers all his evil gain
The miser in such dreams would rise and shake
Into a beggar's lap; the lying scribe
Would his own lies betray without a bribe.

LXXIII.
The priests would write an explanation full,
Translating hieroglyphics into Greek,
How the God Apis really was a bull,
And nothing more; and bid the herald stick
The same against the temple doors, and pull
The old cant down; they licensed all to speak
What'er they thought of hawks, and cats, and geese,
By pastoral letters to each diocese.

LXXIV.
The king would dress an ape up in his crown
And robes, and seat him on his glorious seat,
And on the right hand of the sunlike throne
Would place a gaudy mock-bird to repeat
The chatterings of the monkey. Every one
Of the prone courtiers crawled to kiss the feet
Of their great Emperor, when the morning came,
And kissed alas, how many kiss the same!

LXXV.
The soldiers dreamed that they were blacksmiths, and
Walked out of quarters in somnambulism;
Round the red anvils you might see them stand
Like Cyclopses in Vulcan's sooty abysm,
Beating their swords to ploughshares; in a band
The jailors sent those of the liberal schism
Free through the streets of Memphis, much, I was,
To the annoyance of king Amasis.

LXXVI.
And timid lovers who had been so coy,
They hardly knew whether they loved or not,

Would rise out of their rest, and take sweet joy,
To the fulfilment of their inmost thought;
And when next day the maiden and the boy
Met one another, both, like sinners caught,
Blushed at the thing which each believed was done
Only in fancy, till the tenth moon shone;

LXXVII.
And then the Witch would let them take no ill:
Of many thousand schemes which lovers find,
The Witch found one, and so they took their fill
Of happiness in marriage warm and kind.
Friends who, by practice of some envious skill,
Were torn apart, a wide wound, mind from mind!
She did unite again with visions clear
Of deep affection and of truth sincere.

LXXVIII.
These were the pranks she played among the cities
Of mortal men, and what she did to Sprites
And Gods, entangling them in her sweet ditties
To do her will, and show their subtle sleights,
I will declare another time; for it is
A tale more fit for the weird winter nights
Than for these garish summer days, when we
Scarcely believe much more than we can see.


## EPIPSYCHIDION

VERSES ADDRESSED TO THE NOBLE AND UNFORTUNATE LADY, EMILIA V____, NOW IMPRISONED IN THE CONVENT OF _____

L'anima amante si slancia fuori del creato, e si crea nel infinito un Mondo tutto per essa, diverso assai da questo oscuro e pauroso baratro. HER OWN WORDS

[The loving soul launches beyond creation, and creates for itself in the infinite a world all its own, far different from this dark and terrifying gulf". Teresa Viviani]


[I]
Sweet Spirit! Sister of that orphan one,
Whose empire is the name thou weepest on,
In my heart's temple I suspend to thee
These votive wreaths of withered memory.

[II]
Poor captive bird! Who, from thy narrow cage,
Pourest such music, that it might assuage
The rugged hearts of those who prisoned thee,
Were they not deaf to all sweet melody;
This song shall be thy rose: its petals pale
Are dead, indeed, my adored Nightingale!
But soft and fragrant is the faded blossom,
And it has no thorn left to wound thy bosom.


[III]
High, spirit-winged Heart! Who dost for over
Beat thine unfeeling bars with vain endeavour,
'Till those bright plumes of thought, in which arrayed
It over-soared this low and worldly shade,
Lie shattered; and thy panting wounded breast
Stains with dear blood its unmaternal nest!
I weep vain tears: blood would less bitter be,
Yet poured forth gladlier, could it profit thee


[IV]
Seraph of Heaven! Too gentle to be human,
Veiling beneath that radiant form of Woman
All that is insupportable in thee
Of light, and love, and immortality!
Sweet Benediction in the eternal Curse!
Veiled Glory of this lampless Universe!
Thou Moon beyond the clouds! Thou living Form
Among the Dead! Thou Star above the Storm!
Thou Wonder, and thou Beauty, and thou Terror!
Thou Harmony of Nature's art! Thou Mirror
In whom, as in the splendour of the Sun
All shapes look glorious which thou gazest on!
Aye, even the dim words which obscure thee now
Flash, lightning-like, with unaccustomed glow;
I pray thee that thou blot from this sad song
All of its much mortality and wrong,
With those clear drops, which start like sacred dew
From the twin lights thy sweet soul darkens through,
Weeping, till sorrow becomes ecstasy:
Then smile on it, so that it may not die.


[V]
I never thought before my death to see

Youth's vision thus made perfect. Emily,
I love thee; though the world by no thin name
Will hide that love from its unvalued shame.
Would we two had been twins of the same mother!
Or that the name my heart lent to another
Could be a sister's bond for her and thee,
Blending two beams of one eternity!
Yet were one lawful and the other true,
These names, though dear, could paint not, as is due,
How beyond refuge I am thine. Ah me!
I am not thine: I am a part of thee.


[VI]
Sweet Lamp! My moth-like Muse has burnt its wings;
Or, like a dying swan who soars and sings,
Young Love should teach Time, in his own grey style,
All that thou art. Art thou not void of guile,
A lovely soul formed to be blest and bless?
A well of sealed and secret happiness,
Whose waters like blithe light and music are,
Vanquishing dissonance and gloom? A Star
Which moves not in the moving Heavens, alone?
A smile amid dark frowns? a gentle tone
Amid rude voices? a beloved light?
A Solitude, a Refuge, a Delight?
A lute, which those whom love has taught to play
Make music on, to soothe the roughest day
And lull fond grief asleep? A buried treasure?
A cradle of young thoughts of wingless pleasure?
A violet-shrouded grave of Woe?–I measure
The world of fancies, seeking one like thee,
And find–alas! Mine own infirmity.


[VII]
She met me Stranger, upon life's rough way,
And lured me towards sweet Death; as Night by Day,
Winter by Spring, or Sorrow by swift Hope,
Led into light, life, peace. An antelope,
In the suspended impulse of its lightness,
Were less ethereally light: the brightness
Of her divinest presence trembles through
Her limbs, as underneath a cloud of dew
Embodied in the windless Heaven of June
Amid the splendour-winged stars, the Moon
Burns, inextinguishably beautiful:

And from her lips, as from a hyacinth full
Of honey-dew, a liquid murmur drops,
Killing the sense with passion; sweet as stops
Of planetary music heard in trance.
In her mild lights the starry spirits dance,
The sun-beams of those wells which ever leap
Under the lightnings of the soul-too deep
For the brief fathom-line of thought or sense
The glory of her being, issuing thence,
Stains the dead, blank, cold air with a warm shade
Of unentangled intermixture, made
By Love, of light and motion: one intense
Diffusion, one serene Omnipresence
Whose flowing outlines mingle in their flowing
Around her cheeks and utmost fingers glowing
With the unintermitted blood, which there
Quivers, (as in a fleece of snow-like air
The crimson pulse of living morning quiver,)
Continuously prolonged, and ending never
Till they are lose, and in that Beauty furled
Which penetrates and clasps and fills the world;
Scarce visible from extreme loveliness.
Warm fragrance seems to fall from her light dress,
And her loose hair; and where some heavy tress
The air of her own speed has disentwined,
The sweetness seems to satiate the faint wind;
And in the soul a wild odour is felt,
Beyond the sense, like fiery dews that melt
Into the bosom of a frozen bud.
See where she stands! A mortal shape indued
With love and life and light and deity,
And motion which may change but cannot die;
An image of some bright Eternity;
A shadow of some golden dream; a Splendour
Leaving the third sphere pilotless; a tender
Reflection of the eternal Moon of Love
Under whose motions life's dull billows move;
A Metaphor of Spring and Youth and Morning;
A vision like incarnate April, warning,
With smiles and tears, Frost the Anatomy
Into his summer grave.

[VIII]
Ah, woe is me!
What have I dared? Where am I lifted? How
Shall I descend, and perish not? I know

That Love makes all things equal: I have heard
By mine own heart this joyous truth averred:
The spirit of the worm beneath the sod
In love and worship, blends itself with God.


[IX]
Spouse! Sister! Angel! Pilot of the Fate
Whose course has been so starless! O too late
Beloved! O too soon adored, by me!
For in the fields of immortality
My spirit should at first have worshipped thine,
A divine presence in a place divine;
Or should have moved beside it on this earth,
A shadow of that substance, from its birth;
But not as now: I love thee; yes, I feel
That on the fountain of my heart a seal
Is set, to keep its waters pure and bright
For thee, since in those tears thou hast delight.
We-are we not formed, as notes of music are,
For one another, though dissimilar;
such difference without discord, as can make
Those sweetest sounds, in which all spirits shake
As trembling leaves in a continuous air?


[X]
Thy wisdom speaks in me, and bids me dare
Beacon the rocks on which high hearts are wreckt.
I never was attached to that great sect,
Whose doctrine is, that each one should select
Out of the crowd a mistress or a friend,
And all the rest, though fair and wise, commend
To cold oblivion, though it is in the code
Of modern morals, and the beaten road
Which those poor slaves with weary footsteps tread,
Who travel to their home among the dead
By the broad highway of the world, and so
With one chained friend, perhaps a jealous foe,
The dreariest and the longest journey go.


[XI]
True Love in this differs from gold and clay,
That to divide is not to take away.
Love is like understanding, that grows bright,
Gazing on many truths; 'tis like thy light,

Imagination! which from earth and sky,
And from the depths of human phantasy,
As from a thousand prisms and mirrors, fills
The Universe with glorious beams, and kills
Error, the worm, with many a sun-like arrow
Of its reverberated lightning. Narrow
The heart that loves, the brain that contemplates,
The life that wears,
the spirit that creates
One object, and one form, and builds thereby
A sepulchre for its eternity.


[XII]
Mind from its object differs most in this:
Evil from good; misery from happiness;
The baser from the nobler; the impure
And frail, from what is clear and must endure.
If you divide suffering and dross, you may
Diminish till it is consumed away;
If you divide pleasure and love and thought,
Each part exceeds the whole; and we know not
How much, while any yet remains unshared,
Of pleasure may be gained, of sorrow spared:
This truth is that deep well, whence sages draw
The unenvied light of hope; the eternal law
By which those live, to whom this world of life
Is as a garden ravaged, and whose strife
Tills for the promise of a later birth
The wilderness of this Elysian earth.


[XIII]
There was a Being whom my spirit oft
Met on its visioned wanderings, far aloft,
In the clear golden prime of my youth's dawn,
Upon the fairy isles of sunny lawn,
Amid the enchanted mountains, and the caves
Of divine sleep, and on the air-like waves
Of wonder-level dream, whose tremulous floor
Paved her light steps; - on an imagined shore,
Under the grey break of some promontory
She met me, robed in such exceeding glory
That I beheld her not. In solitudes
Her voice came to me through the whispering woods,
And from the fountains, and the odours deep
Of flowers, which, like lips murmuring in their sleep

Of the sweet kisses which had lulled them there,
Breathed but of her to the enamoured air;
And from the breezes whether low or loud,
And from the rain of every passing cloud,
And from the singing of the summer-birds,
And from all sounds, all silence. In the words
Of antique verse and high romance,-in form,
Sound, colour-in whatever checks that Storm
Which with the shattered present chokes the past;
And in that best philosophy, whose taste
Makes this cold common hell, our life, a doom
As glorious as a fiery martyrdom;
Her Spirit was the harmony of truth.


[XIV]
Then, from the caverns of my dreamy youth
I sprang, as one sandalled with plumes of fire,
And towards the loadstar of my one desire,
I flitted, like a dizzy moth, whose flight
Is as a dead leaf's in the owlet light,
When it would seek in Hesper's setting sphere
A radiant death, a fiery sepulchre,
As if it were a lamp of earthly flame.

But She, whom prayers or tears then could not tame,
Past, like a God throned on a winged plant
Whose burning plumes to tenfold swiftness fan it
Into the dreary cone of our life's shade;
And as a man with mighty loss dismayed,
I would have followed, though the grave between
Yawned like a gulph whose spectres are unseen:
When a voice said:-"O thou of hearts the weakest,
The phantom is beside thee whom thou seekest."
Then I "where?" the world's echo answered "where!"
And in that silence, and in my despair,
I questioned every tongueless wind that flew
Over my tower of mourning, if it knew
Whither 'twas fled, this soul out of my soul;
And murmured names and spells which have control
Over the sightless tyrants of our fate;
But neither prayer nor verse could dissipate
The night which closed on her; nor uncreate
That world within this Chaos, mine and me,
Of which she was the veiled Divinity
The world I say of thoughts that worshipped her:
And therefore I went forth, with hope and fear

And every gentle passion sick to death
Feeding y course with expectation's breath,
Into the wintry forest of our life;
And struggling through its error with vain strife,
And stumbling in my weakness and my haste,
And half bewildered by new forms, I past
Seeking among those untaught foresters
If I could fine one form resembling hers
In which she might has masked herself from me.
There-One, whose voice was venomed melody
Sate by a well, under blue night-shade bowers
The breath of her false mouth was like faint flowers,
Her touch was as electric poison, flame
Out of her looks into my vitals came
And from her living cheeks and bosom flew
A killing air, which pierced like honey-dew
Into the core of my green heart, and lay
Upon its leaves; until, as hair grown grey
O'er a young brow, they hid its unblown prime
With ruins of unseasonable time.


[XV]
In many mortal forms I rashly sought
The shadow of that idol of my thought.
And some were fair-but beauty dies away:
Others were wise-but honeyed words betray:
And One was true-oh! Why not true to me?
Then, as a hunted deer that could not flee,
I turned upon my thoughts, and stood at bay,
Wounded and weak and panting; the cold day
Trembled, for pity of my strife and pain.
When, like a noon-day dawn, there shone again
Deliverance. One stood on my path who seemed
As like the glorious shape which I had dreamed,
As is the Moon, whose changes ever run
Into themselves, to the eternal Sun;
The cold chaste Moon, the Queen of Heaven's bright isles,
Who makes all beautiful on which she smiles,
That wandering shrine of soft yet icy flame
Whichever is transformed, yet still the same,
And warms not but illumines. Young and fair
As the descended Spirit of that sphere,
She hid me, as the Moon may hide the night
From its own darkness, until all was bright
Between the Heaven and Earth of my calm mind,
And, as a cloud charioted by the wind,

She led me to a cave in that wild place,
And sate beside me, with her downward face
Illumining my slumbers, like the Moon
Waxing and waning o'er Endymion.
And I was laid asleep, spirit and limb
And all my being became bright or dim
As the Moon's image in a summer sea,
According as she smiled or frowned on me;
And there I lay, within a chaste cold bed:
Alas, I then was nor alive nor dead:
For at her silver voice came Death and Life,
Unmindful each of their accustomed strife,
Masked like twin babes, a sister and a brother,
The wandering hopes of one abandoned mother,
And through the cavern without wings they flew,
And cried "Away, he is not of our crew."
I wept, and though it be a dream, I weep.


[XVI]
What storms then shook the ocean of my sleep,
Blotting that Moon, whose pale and waning lips
Then shrank as in the sickness of eclipse;
And how my soul was as a lampless sea,
And who was then its Tempest; and when She,
The Planet of that hour, was quenched, what frost
Crept o'er those waters, 'till from coast to coast
The moving billows of my being fell
Into a death of ice, immoveable;
And then-what earthquakes made it gape and split,
The white Moon smiling all the while on it,
These words conceal:-If not, each word would be
The key of staunchless tears. Weep not for me!


[XVII]
At length, into the obscure Forest came
The Vision I had sought through grief and shame.
Athwart that wintry wilderness of thorns
Flashed from her motion splendour like the Morn's
And from her presence life was radiated
Through the grey earth and breanches bare and dead;
Through the grey earth and branches bare and dead;
So that her way was paved, and roofed above
With flowers as soft as thoughts of budding love;
And music from her respiration spread
Like light, -all other sounds were penetrated

By the small, still, sweet spirit of that sound,
So that the savage winds hung mute around;
And odours warm and fresh fell from her hair
Dissolving the dull cold in the froze air:
Soft as an Incarnation of the Su,
When light is changed to love, this glorious One
Floated into the cavern where I lay,
And called my Spirit, and the dreaming clay
Was lifted by the thing that dreamed below
As smoke by fire, and in her beauty's glow
I stood, and felt the dawn of my long night
Was penetrating me with living light:
I knew it was the Vision veiled from me
So many years-that it was Emily.


[XVIII]
Twin spheres of light who rule this passive Earth,
This world of love, this me; and into this birth
Awaken all its fruits and flowers, and dart
Magnetic might into its central heart;
And lift its billows and its mists, and guide
By everlasting laws, each wind and tide
To its fit cloud, and its appointed cave;
And lull its storms, each in the craggy grave
Which was its cradle, luring to faint bowers
The armies of the rainbow-winged showers;
And, as those married lights, which from the towers
Of Heaven look forth and fold the wandering globe
In liquid sleep and splendour, as a robe;
And all their many-mingled influence blend,
If equal, yet unlike, to one sweet end;
So ye, bright regents, with alternate sway
Govern my sphere of being, night and day!
Thou, not disdaining even a borrowed might;
Thou, not eclipsing a remoter light;
And though the shadow of the seasons three,
From Spring to Autumn's sere maturity,
Light it into the Winter of the tomb,
Where it may ripen to a brighter bloom
Thou too, O Comet beautiful and fience,
Who drew the heart of this frail Universe
Towards thine own, till, wreckt in that convulsion,
Alternating attraction and repulsion,
Thine went astray and taht wast rent in twain;
Oh, float into our azure heaven again!
Be there love's folding-star at thy return;

The living Sun will feed thee from its urn
Of golden fire; the Moon will veil her horn
In thy last smiles; adoring Even and Morn
Will worship thee with incense of calm breath
And lights and shadows; as the star of Death
And Birth, is worshipped by those sisters wild
Called Hope and Fear-upon the heart are piled
Their offerings,-of this sacrifice divine
A World shall be the altar.


[XIX]
Lady mine,
Scorn not these flowers of thought, the fading birth
Which from its heart of hearts that plant puts forth
Whose fruit, made perfect by thy sunny eyes,
Will be as of the trees of Paradise.


[XX]
The day is come, and thou wilt fly with me.
To whatsoe'er of dull mortality
Is mine, remain a vestal sister still;
To the intense, the deep, the imperishable,
Not mine but me, henceforth be thou united
Even as a bride, delighting and delighted.
The hour is come:-the destined Star has risen
Which shall descend upon a vacant prison.
The walls are high, the gates are strong, thick set
The sentinels-but true love never yet
Was thus constrained: it overleaps all fence:
Like lightning, with invisible violence
Piercing its continents; like Heaven's free breath,
Which he who grasps can hold not; liker Death,
Who rides upon a thought, and makes his way
Through temple, tower, and palace, and the array
Of arms: more strength has Love than he or they;
For it can burst his charnel, and make free
The limbs in chains, the heart in agony,
The soul in dust and chaos.


[XXI]
Emily,
A ship is floating in the harbour now,
A wind is hovering o'er the mountain's brow;
There is a path on the sea's azure floor,

No keel has ever plough'd that path before;
The halcyons brood around the foamless isles;
The treacherous Ocean has forsworn its wiles;
The merry mariners are bold and free:
Say, my heart's sister, wilt thou sail with me?
Our bark is as an albatross, whose nest
Is a far Eden of the purple East;
And we between her wings will sit, while Night,
And Day, and Storm, and Calm, pursue their flight,
Our ministers, along the boundless Sea,
Treading each other's heels, unheededly.
It is an isle under Ionian skies,
Beautiful as a wreck of Paradise,
And, for the harbours are not safe and good,
This land would have remain'd a solitude
But for some pastoral people native there,
Who from the Elysian, clear, and golden air
Draw the last spirit of the age of gold,
Simple and spirited; innocent and bold.
The blue Aegean girds this chosen home,
With ever-changing sound and light and foam,
Kissing the sifted sands, and caverns hoar;
And all the winds wandering along the shore
Undulate with the undulating tide:
There are thick woods where sylvan forms abide;
And many a fountain, rivulet and pond,
As clear as elemental diamond,
Or serene morning air; and far beyond,
The mossy tracks made by the goats and deer
(Which the rough shepherd treads but once a year)
Pierce into glades, caverns and bowers, and halls
Built round with ivy, which the waterfalls
Illumining, with sound that never fails
Accompany the noonday nightingales;
And all the place is peopled with sweet airs;
The light clear element which the isle wears
Is heavy with the scent of lemon-flowers,
Which floats like mist laden with unseen showers,
And falls upon the eyelids like faint sleep;
And from the moss violets and jonquils peep
And dart their arrowy odour through the brain
Till you might faint with that delicious pain.
And every motion, odour, beam and tone,
With that deep music is in unison:
Which is a soul within the soul, they seem
Like echoes of an antenatal dream.
It is an isle 'twixt Heaven, Air, Earth and Sea,

Cradled and hung in clear tranquillity;
Bright as that wandering Eden Lucifer,
Wash'd by the soft blue Oceans of young air.
It is a favour'd place. Famine or Blight,
Pestilence, War and Earthquake, never light
Upon its mountain-peaks; blind vultures, they
Sail onward far upon their fatal way:
The wingèèd storms, chanting their thunder-psalm
To other lands, leave azure chasms of calm
Over this isle, or weep themselves in dew,
From which its fields and woods ever renew
Their green and golden immortality.
And from the sea there rise, and from the sky
There fall, clear exhalations, soft and bright,
Veil after veil, each hiding some delight,
Which Sun or Moon or zephyr draw aside,
Till the isle's beauty, like a naked bride
Glowing at once with love and loveliness,
Blushes and trembles at its own excess:
Yet, like a buried lamp, a Soul no less
Burns in the heart of this delicious isle,
An atom of th' Eternal, whose own smile
Unfolds itself, and may be felt not seen
O'er the gray rocks, blue waves and forests green,
Filling their bare and void interstices.
But the chief marvel of the wilderness
Is a lone dwelling, built by whom or how
None of the rustic island-people know:
'Tis not a tower of strength, though with its height
It overtops the woods; but, for delight,
Some wise and tender Ocean-King, ere crime
Had been invented, in the world's young prime,
Rear'd it, a wonder of that simple time,
An envy of the isles, a pleasure-house
Made sacred to his sister and his spouse.
It scarce seems now a wreck of human art,
But, as it were, Titanic; in the heart
Of Earth having assum'd its form, then grown
Out of the mountains, from the living stone,
Lifting itself in caverns light and high:
For all the antique and learned imagery
Has been eras'd, and in the place of it
The ivy and the wild-vine interknit
The volumes of their many-twining stems;
Parasite flowers illume with dewy gems
The lampless halls, and when they fade, the sky
Peeps through their winter-woof of tracery

With moonlight patches, or star atoms keen,
Or fragments of the day's intense serene;
Working mosaic on their Parian floors.
And, day and night, aloof, from the high towers
And terraces, the Earth and Ocean seem
To sleep in one another's arms, and dream
Of waves, flowers, clouds, woods, rocks, and all that we
Read in their smiles, and call reality.

[XXII]
This isle and house are mine, and I have vow'd
Thee to be lady of the solitude.
And I have fitted up some chambers there
Looking towards the golden Eastern air,
And level with the living winds, which flow
Like waves above the living waves below.
I have sent books and music there, and all
Those instruments with which high Spirits call
The future from its cradle, and the past
Out of its grave, and make the present last
In thoughts and joys which sleep, but cannot die,
Folded within their own eternity.
Our simple life wants little, and true taste
Hires not the pale drudge Luxury to waste
The scene it would adorn, and therefore still,
Nature with all her children haunts the hill.
The ring-dove, in the embowering ivy, yet
Keeps up her love-lament, and the owls flit
Round the evening tower, and the young stars glance
Between the quick bats in their twilight dance;
The spotted deer bask in the fresh moonlight
Before our gate, and the slow, silent night
Is measur'd by the pants of their calm sleep.
Be this our home in life, and when years heap
Their wither'd hours, like leaves, on our decay,
Let us become the overhanging day,
The living soul of this Elysian isle,
Conscious, inseparable, one. Meanwhile
We two will rise, and sit, and walk together,
Under the roof of blue Ionian weather,
And wander in the meadows, or ascend
The mossy mountains, where the blue heavens bend
With lightest winds, to touch their paramour;
Or linger, where the pebble-paven shore,
Under the quick, faint kisses of the sea,
Trembles and sparkles as with ecstasy

Possessing and possess'd by all that is
Within that calm circumference of bliss,
And by each other, till to love and live
Be one: or, at the noontide hour, arrive
Where some old cavern hoar seems yet to keep
The moonlight of the expir'd night asleep,
Through which the awaken'd day can never peep;
A veil for our seclusion, close as night's,
Where secure sleep may kill thine innocent lights;
Sleep, the fresh dew of languid love, the rain
Whose drops quench kisses till they burn again.
And we will talk, until thought's melody
Become too sweet for utterance, and it die
In words, to live again in looks, which dart
With thrilling tone into the voiceless heart,
Harmonizing silence without a sound.
Our breath shall intermix, our bosoms bound,
And our veins beat together; and our lips
With other eloquence than words, eclipse
The soul that burns between them, and the wells
Which boil under our being's inmost cells,
The fountains of our deepest life, shall be
Confus'd in Passion's golden purity,
As mountain-springs under the morning sun.
We shall become the same, we shall be one
Spirit within two frames, oh! wherefore two?
One passion in twin-hearts, which grows and grew,
Till like two meteors of expanding flame,
Those spheres instinct with it become the same,
Touch, mingle, are transfigur'd; ever still
Burning, yet ever inconsumable:
In one another's substance finding food,
Like flames too pure and light and unimbu'd
To nourish their bright lives with baser prey,
Which point to Heaven and cannot pass away:
One hope within two wills, one will beneath
Two overshadowing minds, one life, one death,
One Heaven, one Hell, one immortality,
And one annihilation. Woe is me!
The winged words on which my soul would pierce
Into the height of Love's rare Universe,
Are chains of lead around its flight of fire
I pant, I sink, I tremble, I expire!


[XXIII]
Weak verses, go kneel at your Soverign's feet,

And say "We are the masters of thy slave;
What wouldest thou with us and ours and thine?"
Then call your sisters from Oblivion's cave,
And singing loud: "Love's very pain is sweet,
But its reward is in the world divine
Which, if not here, it builds beyond the grave."
So shall ye live when I am there. Then haste
Over the hearts of men, until ye meet
Marina, Vanna, Primus, and the rest,
And bid them love each other and be blest:
And leave the troop which errs, and which reproves,
And come and be my guest, for I am Love's.


## JULIAN AND MADDALO. A CONVERSATION.

Composed at Este after Shelley's first visit to Venice, 1818 (Autumn); first published in the "Posthumous Poems", London, 1824 The date, 'May, 1819,' affixed to "Julian and Maddalo" in the "Posthumous Poems", 1824, indicates the time when the text was finally revised by Shelley.


### PREFACE.
The meadows with fresh streams, the bees with thyme,
The goats with the green leaves of budding Spring,
Are saturated not, nor Love with tears. VIRGIL'S "Gallus".

Count Maddalo is a Venetian nobleman of ancient family and of great fortune, who, without mixing much in the society of his countrymen, resides chiefly at his magnificent palace in that city. He is a person of the most consummate genius, and capable, if he would direct his energies to such an end, of becoming the redeemer of his degraded country. But it is his weakness to be proud: he derives, from a comparison of his own extraordinary mind with the dwarfish intellects that surround him, an intense apprehension of the nothingness of human life. His passions and his powers are incomparably greater than those of other men; and, instead of the latter having been employed in curbing the former, they have mutually lent each other strength. His ambition preys upon itself, for want of objects which it can consider worthy of exertion. I say that Maddalo is proud, because I can find no other word to express the concentred and impatient feelings which consume him; but it is on his own hopes and affections only that he seems to trample, for in social life no human being can be more gentle, patient and unassuming than Maddalo. He is cheerful, frank and witty. His more serious conversation is a sort of intoxication; men are held by it as by a spell. He has travelled much; and there is an inexpressible charm in his relation of his adventures in different countries.

Julian is an Englishman of good family, passionately attached to those philosophical notions which assert the power of man over his own mind, and the immense improvements of which, by the extinction of certain moral superstitions, human society may be yet susceptible. Without concealing the evil in the world he is forever speculating how good may be made superior. He is a complete infidel, and a scoffer at all things reputed holy; and Maddalo takes a wicked pleasure in drawing out his taunts against religion. What Maddalo thinks on these matters is not exactly known. Julian, in spite of his heterodox opinions, is conjectured by his friends to possess some good qualities. How far this is possible the pious reader will determine. Julian is rather serious.

Of the Maniac I can give no information. He seems, by his own account, to have been disappointed in love. He was evidently a very cultivated and amiable person when in his right senses. His story, told at length, might be like many other stories of the same kind: the unconnected exclamations of his agony will perhaps be found a sufficient comment for the text of every heart.

Julian And Maddalo

I rode one evening with Count Maddalo
Upon the bank of land which breaks the flow
Of Adria towards Venice: a bare strand
Of hillocks, heaped from ever-shifting sand,
Matted with thistles and amphibious weeds,
Such as from earth's embrace the salt ooze breeds,
Is this; an uninhabited sea-side,
Which the lone fisher, when his nets are dried,
Abandons; and no other object breaks
The waste, but one dwarf tree and some few stakes
Broken and unrepaired, and the tide makes
A narrow space of level sand thereon,
Where 'twas our wont to ride while day went down.
This ride was my delight. I love all waste
And solitary places; where we taste
The pleasure of believing what we see
Is boundless, as we wish our souls to be:
And such was this wide ocean, and this shore
More barren than its billows; and yet more
Than all, with a remembered friend I love
To ride as then I rode; for the winds drove
The living spray along the sunny air
Into our faces; the blue heavens were bare,
Stripped to their depths by the awakening north;
And, from the waves, sound like delight broke forth
Harmonising with solitude, and sent
Into our hearts aereal merriment.
So, as we rode, we talked; and the swift thought,

Winging itself with laughter, lingered not,
But flew from brain to brain, such glee was ours,
Charged with light memories of remembered hours,
None slow enough for sadness: till we came
Homeward, which always makes the spirit tame.
This day had been cheerful but cold, and now
The sun was sinking, and the wind also.
Our talk grew somewhat serious, as may be
Talk interrupted with such raillery
As mocks itself, because it cannot scorn
The thoughts it would extinguish: 'twas forlorn,
Yet pleasing, such as once, so poets tell,
The devils held within the dales of Hell
Concerning God, freewill and destiny:
Of all that earth has been or yet may be,
All that vain men imagine or believe,
Or hope can paint or suffering may achieve,
We descanted; and I (for ever still
Is it not wise to make the best of ill?)
Argued against despondency, but pride
Made my companion take the darker side.
The sense that he was greater than his kind
Had struck, methinks, his eagle spirit blind
By gazing on its own exceeding light.
Meanwhile the sun paused ere it should alight,
Over the horizon of the mountains; Oh,
How beautiful is sunset, when the glow
Of Heaven descends upon a land like thee,
Thou Paradise of exiles, Italy!
Thy mountains, seas and vineyards, and the towers
Of cities they encircle! it was ours
To stand on thee, beholding it: and then,
Just where we had dismounted, the Count's men
Were waiting for us with the gondola.
As those who pause on some delightful way
Though bent on pleasant pilgrimage, we stood
Looking upon the evening, and the flood
Which lay between the city and the shore,
Paved with the image of the sky...the hoar
And aery Alps towards the North appeared
Through mist, an heaven-sustaining bulwark reared
Between the East and West; and half the sky
Was roofed with clouds of rich emblazonry
Dark purple at the zenith, which still grew
Down the steep West into a wondrous hue
Brighter than burning gold, even to the rent
Where the swift sun yet paused in his descent

Among the many-folded hills: they were
Those famous Euganean hills, which bear,
As seen from Lido thro' the harbour piles,
The likeness of a clump of peaked isles
And then, as if the Earth and Sea had been
Dissolved into one lake of fire, were seen
Those mountains towering as from waves of flame
Around the vaporous sun, from which there came
The inmost purple spirit of light, and made
Their very peaks transparent. 'Ere it fade,'
Said my companion, 'I will show you soon
A better station' so, o'er the lagune
We glided; and from that funereal bark
I leaned, and saw the city, and could mark
How from their many isles, in evening's gleam,
Its temples and its palaces did seem
Like fabrics of enchantment piled to Heaven.
I was about to speak, when 'We are even
Now at the point I meant,' said Maddalo,
And bade the gondolieri cease to row.
'Look, Julian, on the west, and listen well
If you hear not a deep and heavy bell.'
I looked, and saw between us and the sun
A building on an island; such a one
As age to age might add, for uses vile,
A windowless, deformed and dreary pile;
And on the top an open tower, where hung
A bell, which in the radiance swayed and swung;
We could just hear its hoarse and iron tongue:
The broad sun sunk behind it, and it tolled
In strong and black relief. 'What we behold
Shall be the madhouse and its belfry tower,'
Said Maddalo, 'and ever at this hour
Those who may cross the water, hear that bell
Which calls the maniacs, each one from his cell,
To vespers.' - 'As much skill as need to pray
In thanks or hope for their dark lot have they
To their stern maker,' I replied. 'O ho!
You talk as in years past,' said Maddalo.
''Tis strange men change not. You were ever still
Among Christ's flock a perilous infidel,
A wolf for the meek lambs, if you can't swim
Beware of Providence.' I looked on him,
But the gay smile had faded in his eye.
'And such,' he cried, 'is our mortality,
And this must be the emblem and the sign
Of what should be eternal and divine!

And like that black and dreary bell, the soul,
Hung in a heaven-illumined tower, must toll
Our thoughts and our desires to meet below
Round the rent heart and pray as madmen do
For what? they know not, till the night of death
As sunset that strange vision, severeth
Our memory from itself, and us from all
We sought and yet were baffled.' I recall
The sense of what he said, although I mar
The force of his expressions. The broad star
Of day meanwhile had sunk behind the hill,
And the black bell became invisible,
And the red tower looked gray, and all between
The churches, ships and palaces were seen
Huddled in gloom; into the purple sea
The orange hues of heaven sunk silently.
We hardly spoke, and soon the gondola
Conveyed me to my lodging by the way.
The following morn was rainy, cold, and dim:
Ere Maddalo arose, I called on him,
And whilst I waited with his child I played;
A lovelier toy sweet Nature never made;
A serious, subtle, wild, yet gentle being,
Graceful without design and unforeseeing,
With eyes, Oh speak not of her eyes! which seem
Twin mirrors of Italian Heaven, yet gleam
With such deep meaning, as we never see
But in the human countenance: with me
She was a special favourite: I had nursed
Her fine and feeble limbs when she came first
To this bleak world; and she yet seemed to know
On second sight her ancient playfellow,
Less changed than she was by six months or so;
For after her first shyness was worn out
We sate there, rolling billiard balls about,
When the Count entered. Salutations past
'The word you spoke last night might well have cast
A darkness on my spirit, if man be
The passive thing you say, I should not see
Much harm in the religions and old saws
(Tho' I may never own such leaden laws)
Which break a teachless nature to the yoke:
Mine is another faith.' thus much I spoke
And noting he replied not, added: 'See
This lovely child, blithe, innocent and free;
She spends a happy time with little care,
While we to such sick thoughts subjected are

As came on you last night. It is our will
That thus enchains us to permitted ill
We might be otherwise, we might be all
We dream of happy, high, majestical.
Where is the love, beauty, and truth we seek,
But in our mind? and if we were not weak
Should we be less in deed than in desire?'
'Ay, if we were not weak and we aspire
How vainly to be strong!' said Maddalo:
'You talk Utopia.' 'It remains to know,'
I then rejoined, 'and those who try may find
How strong the chains are which our spirit bind;
Brittle perchance as straw...We are assured
Much may be conquered, much may be endured,
Of what degrades and crushes us. We know
That we have power over ourselves to do
And suffer what, we know not till we try;
But something nobler than to live and die
So taught those kings of old philosophy
Who reigned, before Religion made men blind;
And those who suffer with their suffering kind
Yet feel their faith, religion.' 'My dear friend,'
Said Maddalo, 'my judgement will not bend
To your opinion, though I think you might
Make such a system refutation-tight
As far as words go. I knew one like you
Who to this city came some months ago,
With whom I argued in this sort, and he
Is now gone mad, and so he answered me,
Poor fellow! but if you would like to go,
We'll visit him, and his wild talk will show
How vain are such aspiring theories.'
'I hope to prove the induction otherwise,
And that a want of that true theory, still,
Which seeks a "soul of goodness" in things ill
Or in himself or others, has thus bowed
His being, there are some by nature proud,
Who patient in all else demand but this
To love and be beloved with gentleness;
And being scorned, what wonder if they die
Some living death? this is not destiny
But man's own wilful ill.'
As thus I spoke
Servants announced the gondola, and we
Through the fast-falling rain and high-wrought sea
Sailed to the island where the madhouse stands.
We disembarked. The clap of tortured hands,

Fierce yells and howlings and lamentings keen,
And laughter where complaint had merrier been,
Moans, shrieks, and curses, and blaspheming prayers
Accosted us. We climbed the oozy stairs
Into an old courtyard. I heard on high,
Then, fragments of most touching melody,
But looking up saw not the singer there
Through the black bars in the tempestuous air
I saw, like weeds on a wrecked palace growing,
Long tangled locks flung wildly forth, and flowing,
Of those who on a sudden were beguiled
Into strange silence, and looked forth and smiled
Hearing sweet sounds. Then I: 'Methinks there were
A cure of these with patience and kind care,
If music can thus move...but what is he
Whom we seek here?' 'Of his sad history
I know but this,' said Maddalo: 'he came
To Venice a dejected man, and fame
Said he was wealthy, or he had been so;
Some thought the loss of fortune wrought him woe;
But he was ever talking in such sort
As you do, far more sadly, he seemed hurt,
Even as a man with his peculiar wrong,
To hear but of the oppression of the strong,
Or those absurd deceits (I think with you
In some respects, you know) which carry through
The excellent impostors of this earth
When they outface detection, he had worth,
Poor fellow! but a humorist in his way'
'Alas, what drove him mad?' 'I cannot say:
A lady came with him from France, and when
She left him and returned, he wandered then
About yon lonely isles of desert sand
Till he grew wild, he had no cash or land
Remaining, the police had brought him here
Some fancy took him and he would not bear
Removal; so I fitted up for him
Those rooms beside the sea, to please his whim,
And sent him busts and books and urns for flowers,
Which had adorned his life in happier hours,
And instruments of music, you may guess
A stranger could do little more or less
For one so gentle and unfortunate:
And those are his sweet strains which charm the weight
From madmen's chains, and make this Hell appear
A heaven of sacred silence, hushed to hear.'
'Nay, this was kind of you, he had no claim,

As the world says', 'None, but the very same
Which I on all mankind were I as he
Fallen to such deep reverse; his melody
Is interrupted, now we hear the din
Of madmen, shriek on shriek, again begin;
Let us now visit him; after this strain
He ever communes with himself again,
And sees nor hears not any.' Having said
These words, we called the keeper, and he led
To an apartment opening on the sea
There the poor wretch was sitting mournfully
Near a piano, his pale fingers twined
One with the other, and the ooze and wind
Rushed through an open casement, and did sway
His hair, and starred it with the brackish spray;
His head was leaning on a music book,
And he was muttering, and his lean limbs shook;
His lips were pressed against a folded leaf
In hue too beautiful for health, and grief
Smiled in their motions as they lay apart
As one who wrought from his own fervid heart
The eloquence of passion, soon he raised
His sad meek face and eyes lustrous and glazed
And spoke, sometimes as one who wrote, and thought
His words might move some heart that heeded not,
If sent to distant lands: and then as one
Reproaching deeds never to be undone
With wondering self-compassion; then his speech
Was lost in grief, and then his words came each
Unmodulated, cold, expressionless,
But that from one jarred accent you might guess
It was despair made them so uniform:
And all the while the loud and gusty storm
Hissed through the window, and we stood behind
Stealing his accents from the envious wind
Unseen. I yet remember what he said
Distinctly: such impression his words made.
'Month after month,' he cried, 'to bear this load
And as a jade urged by the whip and goad
To drag life on, which like a heavy chain
Lengthens behind with many a link of pain!
And not to speak my grief. O, not to dare
To give a human voice to my despair,
But live, and move, and, wretched thing! smile on
As if I never went aside to groan,
And wear this mask of falsehood even to those
Who are most dear not for my own repose

Alas! no scorn or pain or hate could be
So heavy as that falsehood is to me
But that I cannot bear more altered faces
Than needs must be, more changed and cold embraces,
More misery, disappointment, and mistrust
To own me for their father...Would the dust
Were covered in upon my body now!
That the life ceased to toil within my brow!
And then these thoughts would at the least be fled;
Let us not fear such pain can vex the dead.
'What Power delights to torture us? I know
That to myself I do not wholly owe
What now I suffer, though in part I may.
Alas! none strewed sweet flowers upon the way
Where wandering heedlessly, I met pale Pain
My shadow, which will leave me not again
If I have erred, there was no joy in error,
But pain and insult and unrest and terror;
I have not as some do, bought penitence
With pleasure, and a dark yet sweet offence,
For then, if love and tenderness and truth
Had overlived hope's momentary youth,
My creed should have redeemed me from repenting;
But loathed scorn and outrage unrelenting
Met love excited by far other seeming
Until the end was gained...as one from dreaming
Of sweetest peace, I woke, and found my state
Such as it is.
'O Thou, my spirit's mate
Who, for thou art compassionate and wise,
Wouldst pity me from thy most gentle eyes
If this sad writing thou shouldst ever see
My secret groans must be unheard by thee,
Thou wouldst weep tears bitter as blood to know
Thy lost friend's incommunicable woe.
'Ye few by whom my nature has been weighed
In friendship, let me not that name degrade
By placing on your hearts the secret load
Which crushes mine to dust. There is one road
To peace and that is truth, which follow ye!
Love sometimes leads astray to misery.
Yet think not though subdued and I may well
Say that I am subdued, that the full Hell
Within me would infect the untainted breast
Of sacred nature with its own unrest;
As some perverted beings think to find
In scorn or hate a medicine for the mind

Which scorn or hate have wounded. O how vain!
The dagger heals not but may rend again...
Believe that I am ever still the same
In creed as in resolve, and what may tame
My heart, must leave the understanding free,
Or all would sink in this keen agony
Nor dream that I will join the vulgar cry;
Or with my silence sanction tyranny;
Or seek a moment's shelter from my pain
In any madness which the world calls gain,
Ambition or revenge or thoughts as stern
As those which make me what I am; or turn
To avarice or misanthropy or lust...
Heap on me soon, O grave, thy welcome dust!
Till then the dungeon may demand its prey,
And Poverty and Shame may meet and say
Halting beside me on the public way
"That love-devoted youth is ours, let's sit
Beside him, he may live some six months yet."
Or the red scaffold, as our country bends,
May ask some willing victim; or ye friends
May fall under some sorrow which this heart
Or hand may share or vanquish or avert;
I am prepared, in truth, with no proud joy
To do or suffer aught, as when a boy
I did devote to justice and to love
My nature, worthless now!...
'I must remove
A veil from my pent mind. 'Tis torn aside!
O, pallid as Death's dedicated bride,
Thou mockery which art sitting by my side,
Am I not wan like thee? at the grave's call
I haste, invited to thy wedding-ball
To greet the ghastly paramour, for whom
Thou hast deserted me...and made the tomb
Thy bridal bed...But I beside your feet
Will lie and watch ye from my winding-sheet
Thus...wide awake tho' dead...yet stay, O stay!
Go not so soon, I know not what I say
Hear but my reasons...I am mad, I fear,
My fancy is o'erwrought...thou art not here...
Pale art thou, 'tis most true...but thou art gone,
Thy work is finished...I am left alone!

'Nay, was it I who wooed thee to this breast
Which, like a serpent, thou envenomest
As in repayment of the warmth it lent?

Didst thou not seek me for thine own content?
Did not thy love awaken mine? I thought
That thou wert she who said, "You kiss me not
Ever, I fear you do not love me now"
In truth I loved even to my overthrow
Her, who would fain forget these words: but they
Cling to her mind, and cannot pass away.

'You say that I am proud that when I speak
My lip is tortured with the wrongs which break
The spirit it expresses...Never one
Humbled himself before, as I have done!
Even the instinctive worm on which we tread
Turns, though it wound not then with prostrate head
Sinks in the dusk and writhes like me and dies?
No: wears a living death of agonies!
As the slow shadows of the pointed grass
Mark the eternal periods, his pangs pass,
Slow, ever-moving, making moments be
As mine seem, each an immortality!

'That you had never seen me, never heard
My voice, and more than all had ne'er endured
The deep pollution of my loathed embrace
That your eyes ne'er had lied love in my face
That, like some maniac monk, I had torn out
The nerves of manhood by their bleeding root
With mine own quivering fingers, so that ne'er
Our hearts had for a moment mingled there
To disunite in horror, these were not
With thee, like some suppressed and hideous thought
Which flits athwart our musings, but can find
No rest within a pure and gentle mind...
Thou sealedst them with many a bare broad word,
And searedst my memory o'er them, for I heard
And can forget not...they were ministered
One after one, those curses. Mix them up
Like self-destroying poisons in one cup,
And they will make one blessing which thou ne'er
Didst imprecate for, on me, death.

'It were
A cruel punishment for one most cruel,
If such can love, to make that love the fuel
Of the mind's hell; hate, scorn, remorse, despair:
But ME, whose heart a stranger's tear might wear
As water-drops the sandy fountain-stone,

Who loved and pitied all things, and could moan
For woes which others hear not, and could see
The absent with the glance of phantasy,
And with the poor and trampled sit and weep,
Following the captive to his dungeon deep;
ME, who am as a nerve o'er which do creep
The else unfelt oppressions of this earth,
And was to thee the flame upon thy hearth,
When all beside was cold, that thou on me
Shouldst rain these plagues of blistering agony
Such curses are from lips once eloquent
With love's too partial praise, let none relent
Who intend deeds too dreadful for a name
Henceforth, if an example for the same
They seek...for thou on me lookedst so, and so
And didst speak thus...and thus...I live to show
How much men bear and die not!

'Thou wilt tell
With the grimace of hate, how horrible
It was to meet my love when thine grew less;
Thou wilt admire how I could e'er address
Such features to love's work...this taunt, though true,
(For indeed Nature nor in form nor hue
Bestowed on me her choicest workmanship)
Shall not be thy defence...for since thy lip
Met mine first, years long past, since thine eye kindled
With soft fire under mine, I have not dwindled
Nor changed in mind or body, or in aught
But as love changes what it loveth not
After long years and many trials.
'How vain
Are words! I thought never to speak again,
Not even in secret, not to mine own heart
But from my lips the unwilling accents start,
And from my pen the words flow as I write,
Dazzling my eyes with scalding tears...my sight
Is dim to see that charactered in vain
On this unfeeling leaf which burns the brain
And eats into it...blotting all things fair
And wise and good which time had written there.
'Those who inflict must suffer, for they see
The work of their own hearts, and this must be
Our chastisement or recompense. O child!
I would that thine were like to be more mild
For both our wretched sakes...for thine the most
Who feelest already all that thou hast lost

Without the power to wish it thine again;
And as slow years pass, a funereal train
Each with the ghost of some lost hope or friend
Following it like its shadow, wilt thou bend
No thought on my dead memory?

'Alas, love!
Fear me not...against thee I would not move
A finger in despite. Do I not live
That thou mayst have less bitter cause to grieve?
I give thee tears for scorn and love for hate;
And that thy lot may be less desolate
Than his on whom thou tramplest, I refrain
From that sweet sleep which medicines all pain.
Then, when thou speakest of me, never say
"He could forgive not." Here I cast away
All human passions, all revenge, all pride;
I think, speak, act no ill; I do but hide
Under these words, like embers, every spark
Of that which has consumed me, quick and dark
The grave is yawning...as its roof shall cover
My limbs with dust and worms under and over
So let Oblivion hide this grief...the air
Closes upon my accents, as despair
Upon my heart, let death upon despair!'
He ceased, and overcome leant back awhile,
Then rising, with a melancholy smile
Went to a sofa, and lay down, and slept
A heavy sleep, and in his dreams he wept
And muttered some familiar name, and we
Wept without shame in his society.
I think I never was impressed so much;
The man who were not, must have lacked a touch
Of human nature...then we lingered not,
Although our argument was quite forgot,
But calling the attendants, went to dine
At Maddalo's; yet neither cheer nor wine
Could give us spirits, for we talked of him
And nothing else, till daylight made stars dim;
And we agreed his was some dreadful ill
Wrought on him boldly, yet unspeakable,
By a dear friend; some deadly change in love
Of one vowed deeply which he dreamed not of;
For whose sake he, it seemed, had fixed a blot
Of falsehood on his mind which flourished not
But in the light of all-beholding truth;
And having stamped this canker on his youth

She had abandoned him, and how much more
Might be his woe, we guessed not, he had store
Of friends and fortune once, as we could guess
From his nice habits and his gentleness;
These were now lost...it were a grief indeed
If he had changed one unsustaining reed
For all that such a man might else adorn.
The colours of his mind seemed yet unworn;
For the wild language of his grief was high,
Such as in measure were called poetry;
And I remember one remark which then
Maddalo made. He said: 'Most wretched men
Are cradled into poetry by wrong,
They learn in suffering what they teach in song.'
If I had been an unconnected man,
I, from this moment, should have formed some plan
Never to leave sweet Venice, for to me
It was delight to ride by the lone sea;
And then, the town is silent, one may write
Or read in gondolas by day or night,
Having the little brazen lamp alight,
Unseen, uninterrupted; books are there,
Pictures, and casts from all those statues fair
Which were twin-born with poetry, and all
We seek in towns, with little to recall
Regrets for the green country. I might sit
In Maddalo's great palace, and his wit
And subtle talk would cheer the winter night
And make me know myself, and the firelight
Would flash upon our faces, till the day
Might dawn and make me wonder at my stay:
But I had friends in London too: the chief
Attraction here, was that I sought relief
From the deep tenderness that maniac wrought
Within me, 'twas perhaps an idle thought
But I imagined that if day by day
I watched him, and but seldom went away,
And studied all the beatings of his heart
With zeal, as men study some stubborn art
For their own good, and could by patience find
An entrance to the caverns of his mind,
I might reclaim him from this dark estate:
In friendships I had been most fortunate
Yet never saw I one whom I would call
More willingly my friend; and this was all
Accomplished not; such dreams of baseless good
Oft come and go in crowds or solitude

And leave no trace but what I now designed
Made for long years impression on my mind.
The following morning, urged by my affairs,
I left bright Venice.
After many years
And many changes I returned; the name
Of Venice, and its aspect, was the same;
But Maddalo was travelling far away
Among the mountains of Armenia.
His dog was dead. His child had now become
A woman; such as it has been my doom
To meet with few, a wonder of this earth,
Where there is little of transcendent worth,
Like one of Shakespeare's women: kindly she,
And, with a manner beyond courtesy,
Received her father's friend; and when I asked
Of the lorn maniac, she her memory tasked,
And told as she had heard the mournful tale:
'That the poor sufferer's health began to fail
Two years from my departure, but that then
The lady who had left him, came again.
Her mien had been imperious, but she now
Looked meek, perhaps remorse had brought her low.
Her coming made him better, and they stayed
Together at my father's, for I played,
As I remember, with the lady's shawl
I might be six years old but after all
She left him.'...'Why, her heart must have been tough:
How did it end?' 'And was not this enough?
They met, they parted.' 'Child, is there no more?'
'Something within that interval which bore
The stamp of WHY they parted, HOW they met:
Yet if thine aged eyes disdain to wet
Those wrinkled cheeks with youth's remembered tears,
Ask me no more, but let the silent years
Be closed and cered over their memory
As yon mute marble where their corpses lie.'
I urged and questioned still, she told me how
All happened but the cold world shall not know.


ALASTOR: OR, THE SPIRIT OF SOLITUDE.

[Composed at Bishopsgate Heath, near Windsor Park, autumn, 1815 )

PREFACE.

The poem entitled "Alastor" may be considered as allegorical of one of the most interesting situations of the human mind. It represents a youth of uncorrupted feelings and adventurous genius led forth by an imagination inflamed and purified through familiarity with all that is excellent and majestic, to the contemplation of the universe. He drinks deep of the fountains of knowledge, and is still insatiate. The magnificence and beauty of the external world sinks profoundly into the frame of his conceptions, and affords to their modifications at variety not to be exhausted. so long as it is possible for his desires to point towards objects thus infinite and unmeasured, he is joyous, and tranquil, and self-possessed. But the period arrives when these objects cease to suffice. His mind is at length suddenly awakened and thirsts for intercourse with an intelligence similar to itself. He images to himself the Being whom he loves. Conversant with speculations of the sublimest and most perfect natures, the vision in which he embodies his own imaginations unites all of wonderful, or wise, or beautiful, which the poet, the philosopher, or the lover could depicture. The intellectual faculties, the imagination, the functions of sense, have their respective requisitions on the sympathy of corresponding powers in other human beings. The Poet is represented as uniting these requisitions, and attaching them to a single image. He seeks in vain for a prototype of his conception. Blasted by his disappointment, he descends to an untimely grave.

The picture is not barren of instruction to actual men. The Poet's self-centred seclusion was avenged by the furies of an irresistible passion pursuing him to speedy ruin. But that Power which strikes the luminaries of the world with sudden darkness and extinction, by awakening them to too exquisite a perception of its influences, dooms to a slow and poisonous decay those manner spirits that dare to abjure its dominion. Their destiny is more abject and inglorious as their delinquency is more contemptible and pernicious. They who, deluded by no generous error, instigated by no sacred thirst of doubtful knowledge, duped by no illustrious superstition, loving nothing on this earth, and cherishing no hopes beyond, yet keep aloof from sympathies with their kind, rejoicing neither in human joy nor mourning with human grief; these, and such as they, have their apportioned curse. They languish, because none feel with them their common nature. They are morally dead. They are neither friends, nor lovers, nor fathers, nor citizens of the world, nor benefactors of their country. Among those who attempt to exist without human sympathy, the pure and tender-hearted perish through the intensity and passion of their search after its communities, when the vacancy of their spirit suddenly makes itself felt. All else, selfish, blind, and torpid, are those unforeseeing multitudes who constitute, together with their own, the lasting misery and loneliness of the world. Those who love not their fellow-beings live unfruitful lives, and prepare for their old age a miserable grave.

'The good die first,
And those whose hearts are dry as summer dust,
Burn to the socket!'

December 14, 1815.

ALASTOR: OR, THE SPIRIT OF SOLITUDE.

Earth, Ocean, Air, beloved brotherhood!
If our great Mother has imbued my soul
With aught of natural piety to feel
Your love, and recompense the boon with mine;
If dewy morn, and odorous noon, and even,
With sunset and its gorgeous ministers,
And solemn midnight's tingling silentness;
If autumn's hollow sighs in the sere wood,
And winter robing with pure snow and crowns
Of starry ice the grey grass and bare boughs;
If spring's voluptuous pantings when she breathes
Her first sweet kisses, have been dear to me;
If no bright bird, insect, or gentle beast
I consciously have injured, but still loved
And cherished these my kindred; then forgive
This boast, beloved brethren, and withdraw
No portion of your wonted favour now!

Mother of this unfathomable world!
Favour my solemn song, for I have loved
Thee ever, and thee only; I have watched
Thy shadow, and the darkness of thy steps,
And my heart ever gazes on the depth
Of thy deep mysteries. I have made my bed
In charnels and on coffins, where black death
Keeps record of the trophies won from thee,
Hoping to still these obstinate questionings
Of thee and thine, by forcing some lone ghost,
Thy messenger, to render up the tale
Of what we are. In lone and silent hours,
When night makes a weird sound of its own stillness,
Like an inspired and desperate alchymist
Staking his very life on some dark hope,
Have I mixed awful talk and asking looks
With my most innocent love, until strange tears,
Uniting with those breathless kisses, made
Such magic as compels the charmed night
To render up thy charge:...and, though ne'er yet
Thou hast unveiled thy inmost sanctuary,
Enough from incommunicable dream,
And twilight phantasms, and deep noon-day thought,
Has shone within me, that serenely now
And moveless, as a long-forgotten lyre
Suspended in the solitary dome
Of some mysterious and deserted fane,

I wait thy breath, Great Parent, that my strain
May modulate with murmurs of the air,
And motions of the forests and the sea,
And voice of living beings, and woven hymns
Of night and day, and the deep heart of man.

There was a Poet whose untimely tomb
No human hands with pious reverence reared,
But the charmed eddies of autumnal winds
Built o'er his mouldering bones a pyramid
Of mouldering leaves in the waste wilderness:
A lovely youth, no mourning maiden decked
With weeping flowers, or votive cypress wreath,
The lone couch of his everlasting sleep:
Gentle, and brave, and generous, no lorn bard
Breathed o'er his dark fate one melodious sigh:
He lived, he died, he sung in solitude.
Strangers have wept to hear his passionate notes,
And virgins, as unknown he passed, have pined
And wasted for fond love of his wild eyes.
The fire of those soft orbs has ceased to burn,
And Silence, too enamoured of that voice,
Locks its mute music in her rugged cell.

By solemn vision, and bright silver dream
His infancy was nurtured. Every sight
And sound from the vast earth and ambient air,
Sent to his heart its choicest impulses.
The fountains of divine philosophy
Fled not his thirsting lips, and all of great,
Or good, or lovely, which the sacred past
In truth or fable consecrates, he felt
And knew. When early youth had passed, he left
His cold fireside and alienated home
To seek strange truths in undiscovered lands.
Many a wide waste and tangled wilderness
Has lured his fearless steps; and he has bought
With his sweet voice and eyes, from savage men,
His rest and food. Nature's most secret steps
He like her shadow has pursued, where'er
The red volcano overcanopies
Its fields of snow and pinnacles of ice
With burning smoke, or where bitumen lakes
On black bare pointed islets ever beat
With sluggish surge, or where the secret caves,
Rugged and dark, winding among the springs
Of fire and poison, inaccessible

To avarice or pride, their starry domes
Of diamond and of gold expand above
Numberless and immeasurable halls,
Frequent with crystal column, and clear shrines
Of pearl, and thrones radiant with chrysolite.
Nor had that scene of ampler majesty
Than gems or gold, the varying roof of heaven
And the green earth lost in his heart its claims
To love and wonder; he would linger long
In lonesome vales, making the wild his home,
Until the doves and squirrels would partake
From his innocuous hand his bloodless food,
Lured by the gentle meaning of his looks,
And the wild antelope, that starts whene'er
The dry leaf rustles in the brake, suspend
Her timid steps, to gaze upon a form
More graceful than her own.
His wandering step,
Obedient to high thoughts, has visited
The awful ruins of the days of old:
Athens, and Tyre, and Balbec, and the waste
Where stood Jerusalem, the fallen towers
Of Babylon, the eternal pyramids,
Memphis and Thebes, and whatsoe'er of strange,
Sculptured on alabaster obelisk,
Or jasper tomb, or mutilated sphynx,
Dark Aethiopia in her desert hills
Conceals. Among the ruined temples there,
Stupendous columns, and wild images
Of more than man, where marble daemons watch
The Zodiac's brazen mystery, and dead men
Hang their mute thoughts on the mute walls around,
He lingered, poring on memorials
Of the world's youth: through the long burning day
Gazed on those speechless shapes; nor, when the moon
Filled the mysterious halls with floating shades
Suspended he that task, but ever gazed
And gazed, till meaning on his vacant mind
Flashed like strong inspiration, and he saw
The thrilling secrets of the birth of time.

Meanwhile an Arab maiden brought his food,
Her daily portion, from her father's tent,
And spread her matting for his couch, and stole
From duties and repose to tend his steps,
Enamoured, yet not daring for deep awe
To speak her love: and watched his nightly sleep,

Sleepless herself, to gaze upon his lips
Parted in slumber, whence the regular breath
Of innocent dreams arose; then, when red morn
Made paler the pale moon, to her cold home
Wildered, and wan, and panting, she returned.

The Poet, wandering on, through Arabie,
And Persia, and the wild Carmanian waste,
And o'er the aerial mountains which pour down
Indus and Oxus from their icy caves,
In joy and exultation held his way;
Till in the vale of Cashmire, far within
Its loneliest dell, where odorous plants entwine
Beneath the hollow rocks a natural bower,
Beside a sparkling rivulet he stretched
His languid limbs. A vision on his sleep
There came, a dream of hopes that never yet
Had flushed his cheek. He dreamed a veiled maid
Sate near him, talking in low solemn tones.
Her voice was like the voice of his own soul
Heard in the calm of thought; its music long,
Like woven sounds of streams and breezes, held
His inmost sense suspended in its web
Of many-coloured woof and shifting hues.
Knowledge and truth and virtue were her theme,
And lofty hopes of divine liberty,
Thoughts the most dear to him, and poesy,
Herself a poet. Soon the solemn mood
Of her pure mind kindled through all her frame
A permeating fire; wild numbers then
She raised, with voice stifled in tremulous sobs
Subdued by its own pathos; her fair hands
Were bare alone, sweeping from some strange harp
Strange symphony, and in their branching veins
The eloquent blood told an ineffable tale.
The beating of her heart was heard to fill
The pauses of her music, and her breath
Tumultuously accorded with those fits
Of intermitted song. Sudden she rose,
As if her heart impatiently endured
Its bursting burthen: at the sound he turned,
And saw by the warm light of their own life
Her glowing limbs beneath the sinuous veil
Of woven wind, her outspread arms now bare,
Her dark locks floating in the breath of night,
Her beamy bending eyes, her parted lips
Outstretched, and pale, and quivering eagerly.

His strong heart sunk and sickened with excess
Of love. He reared his shuddering limbs and quelled
His gasping breath, and spread his arms to meet
Her panting bosom:...she drew back a while,
Then, yielding to the irresistible joy,
With frantic gesture and short breathless cry
Folded his frame in her dissolving arms.
Now blackness veiled his dizzy eyes, and night
Involved and swallowed up the vision; sleep,
Like a dark flood suspended in its course,
Rolled back its impulse on his vacant brain.

Roused by the shock he started from his trance
The cold white light of morning, the blue moon
Low in the west, the clear and garish hills,
The distinct valley and the vacant woods,
Spread round him where he stood. Whither have fled
The hues of heaven that canopied his bower
Of yesternight? The sounds that soothed his sleep,
The mystery and the majesty of Earth,
The joy, the exultation? His wan eyes
Gaze on the empty scene as vacantly
As ocean's moon looks on the moon in heaven.
The spirit of sweet human love has sent
A vision to the sleep of him who spurned
Her choicest gifts. He eagerly pursues
Beyond the realms of dream that fleeting shade;
He overleaps the bounds. Alas! Alas!
Were limbs, and breath, and being intertwined
Thus treacherously? Lost, lost, for ever lost
In the wide pathless desert of dim sleep,
That beautiful shape! Does the dark gate of death
Conduct to thy mysterious paradise,
O Sleep? Does the bright arch of rainbow clouds
And pendent mountains seen in the calm lake,
Lead only to a black and watery depth,
While death's blue vault, with loathliest vapours hung,
Where every shade which the foul grave exhales
Hides its dead eye from the detested day,
Conducts, O Sleep, to thy delightful realms?
This doubt with sudden tide flowed on his heart;
The insatiate hope which it awakened, stung
His brain even like despair.
While daylight held
The sky, the Poet kept mute conference
With his still soul. At night the passion came,
Like the fierce fiend of a distempered dream,

And shook him from his rest, and led him forth
Into the darkness. As an eagle, grasped
In folds of the green serpent, feels her breast
Burn with the poison, and precipitates
Through night and day, tempest, and calm, and cloud,
Frantic with dizzying anguish, her blind flight
O'er the wide aery wilderness: thus driven
By the bright shadow of that lovely dream,
Beneath the cold glare of the desolate night,
Through tangled swamps and deep precipitous dells,
Startling with careless step the moonlight snake,
He fled. Red morning dawned upon his flight,
Shedding the mockery of its vital hues
Upon his cheek of death. He wandered on
Till vast Aornos seen from Petra's steep
Hung o'er the low horizon like a cloud;
Through Balk, and where the desolated tombs
Of Parthian kings scatter to every wind
Their wasting dust, wildly he wandered on,
Day after day a weary waste of hours,
Bearing within his life the brooding care
That ever fed on its decaying flame.
And now his limbs were lean; his scattered hair,
Sered by the autumn of strange suffering
Sung dirges in the wind; his listless hand
Hung like dead bone within its withered skin;
Life, and the lustre that consumed it, shone
As in a furnace burning secretly
From his dark eyes alone. The cottagers,
Who ministered with human charity
His human wants, beheld with wondering awe
Their fleeting visitant. The mountaineer,
Encountering on some dizzy precipice
That spectral form, deemed that the Spirit of wind
With lightning eyes, and eager breath, and feet
Disturbing not the drifted snow, had paused
In its career: the infant would conceal
His troubled visage in his mother's robe
In terror at the glare of those wild eyes,
To remember their strange light in many a dream
Of after-times; but youthful maidens, taught
By nature, would interpret half the woe
That wasted him, would call him with false names
Brother and friend, would press his pallid hand
At parting, and watch, dim through tears, the path
Of his departure from their father's door.

At length upon the lone Chorasmian shore
He paused, a wide and melancholy waste
Of putrid marshes. A strong impulse urged
His steps to the sea-shore. A swan was there,
Beside a sluggish stream among the reeds.
It rose as he approached, and, with strong wings
Scaling the upward sky, bent its bright course
High over the immeasurable main.
His eyes pursued its flight: 'Thou hast a home,
Beautiful bird; thou voyagest to thine home,
Where thy sweet mate will twine her downy neck
With thine, and welcome thy return with eyes
Bright in the lustre of their own fond joy.
And what am I that I should linger here,
With voice far sweeter than thy dying notes,
Spirit more vast than thine, frame more attuned
To beauty, wasting these surpassing powers
In the deaf air, to the blind earth, and heaven
That echoes not my thoughts?' A gloomy smile
Of desperate hope wrinkled his quivering lips.
For sleep, he knew, kept most relentlessly
Its precious charge, and silent death exposed,
Faithless perhaps as sleep, a shadowy lure,
With doubtful smile mocking its own strange charms.

Startled by his own thoughts he looked around.
There was no fair fiend near him, not a sight
Or sound of awe but in his own deep mind.
A little shallop floating near the shore
Caught the impatient wandering of his gaze.
It had been long abandoned, for its sides
Gaped wide with many a rift, and its frail joints
Swayed with the undulations of the tide.
A restless impulse urged him to embark
And meet lone Death on the drear ocean's waste;
For well he knew that mighty Shadow loves
The slimy caverns of the populous deep.

The day was fair and sunny; sea and sky
Drank its inspiring radiance, and the wind
Swept strongly from the shore, blackening the waves.
Following his eager soul, the wanderer
Leaped in the boat, he spread his cloak aloft
On the bare mast, and took his lonely seat,
And felt the boat speed o'er the tranquil sea
Like a torn cloud before the hurricane.

As one that in a silver vision floats
Obedient to the sweep of odorous winds
Upon resplendent clouds, so rapidly
Along the dark and ruffled waters fled
The straining boat. A whirlwind swept it on,
With fierce gusts and precipitating force,
Through the white ridges of the chafed sea.
The waves arose. Higher and higher still
Their fierce necks writhed beneath the tempest's scourge
Like serpents struggling in a vulture's grasp.
Calm and rejoicing in the fearful war
Of wave ruining on wave, and blast on blast
Descending, and black flood on whirlpool driven
With dark obliterating course, he sate:
As if their genii were the ministers
Appointed to conduct him to the light
Of those beloved eyes, the Poet sate,
Holding the steady helm. Evening came on,
The beams of sunset hung their rainbow hues
High 'mid the shifting domes of sheeted spray
That canopied his path o'er the waste deep;
Twilight, ascending slowly from the east,
Entwined in duskier wreaths her braided locks
O'er the fair front and radiant eyes of day;
Night followed, clad with stars. On every side
More horribly the multitudinous streams
Of ocean's mountainous waste to mutual war
Rushed in dark tumult thundering, as to mock
The calm and spangled sky. The little boat
Still fled before the storm; still fled, like foam
Down the steep cataract of a wintry river;
Now pausing on the edge of the riven wave;
Now leaving far behind the bursting mass
That fell, convulsing ocean: safely fled
As if that frail and wasted human form,
Had been an elemental god.

At midnight
The moon arose; and lo! the ethereal cliffs
Of Caucasus, whose icy summits shone
Among the stars like sunlight, and around
Whose caverned base the whirlpools and the waves
Bursting and eddying irresistibly
Rage and resound forever. Who shall save?
The boat fled on, the boiling torrent drove,
The crags closed round with black and jagged arms,
The shattered mountain overhung the sea,

And faster still, beyond all human speed,
Suspended on the sweep of the smooth wave,
The little boat was driven. A cavern there
Yawned, and amid its slant and winding depths
Ingulfed the rushing sea. The boat fled on
With unrelaxing speed. 'Vision and Love!'
The Poet cried aloud, 'I have beheld
The path of thy departure. Sleep and death
Shall not divide us long.'

The boat pursued
The windings of the cavern. Daylight shone
At length upon that gloomy river's flow;
Now, where the fiercest war among the waves
Is calm, on the unfathomable stream
The boat moved slowly. Where the mountain, riven,
Exposed those black depths to the azure sky,
Ere yet the flood's enormous volume fell
Even to the base of Caucasus, with sound
That shook the everlasting rocks, the mass
Filled with one whirlpool all that ample chasm:
Stair above stair the eddying waters rose,
Circling immeasurably fast, and laved
With alternating dash the gnarled roots
Of mighty trees, that stretched their giant arms
In darkness over it. I' the midst was left,
Reflecting, yet distorting every cloud,
A pool of treacherous and tremendous calm.
Seized by the sway of the ascending stream,
With dizzy swiftness, round, and round, and round,
Ridge after ridge the straining boat arose,
Till on the verge of the extremest curve,
Where, through an opening of the rocky bank,
The waters overflow, and a smooth spot
Of glassy quiet mid those battling tides
Is left, the boat paused shuddering. Shall it sink
Down the abyss? Shall the reverting stress
Of that resistless gulf embosom it?
Now shall it fall? A wandering stream of wind,
Breathed from the west, has caught the expanded sail,
And, lo! with gentle motion, between banks
Of mossy slope, and on a placid stream,
Beneath a woven grove it sails, and, hark!
The ghastly torrent mingles its far roar,
With the breeze murmuring in the musical woods.
Where the embowering trees recede, and leave
A little space of green expanse, the cove

Is closed by meeting banks, whose yellow flowers
For ever gaze on their own drooping eyes,
Reflected in the crystal calm. The wave
Of the boat's motion marred their pensive task,
Which naught but vagrant bird, or wanton wind,
Or falling spear-grass, or their own decay
Had e'er disturbed before. The Poet longed
To deck with their bright hues his withered hair,
But on his heart its solitude returned,
And he forbore. Not the strong impulse hid
In those flushed cheeks, bent eyes, and shadowy frame
Had yet performed its ministry: it hung
Upon his life, as lightning in a cloud
Gleams, hovering ere it vanish, ere the floods
Of night close over it.
The noonday sun
Now shone upon the forest, one vast mass
Of mingling shade, whose brown magnificence
A narrow vale embosoms. There, huge caves,
Scooped in the dark base of their aery rocks,
Mocking its moans, respond and roar forever.
The meeting boughs and implicated leaves
Wove twilight o'er the Poet's path, as led
By love, or dream, or god, or mightier Death,
He sought in Nature's dearest haunt some bank,
Her cradle, and his sepulchre. More dark
And dark the shades accumulate. The oak,
Expanding its immense and knotty arms,
Embraces the light beech. The pyramids
Of the tall cedar overarching frame
Most solemn domes within, and far below,
Like clouds suspended in an emerald sky,
The ash and the acacia floating hang
Tremulous and pale. Like restless serpents, clothed
In rainbow and in fire, the parasites,
Starred with ten thousand blossoms, flow around
The grey trunks, and, as gamesome infants' eyes,
With gentle meanings, and most innocent wiles,
Fold their beams round the hearts of those that love,
These twine their tendrils with the wedded boughs
Uniting their close union; the woven leaves
Make net-work of the dark blue light of day,
And the night's noontide clearness, mutable
As shapes in the weird clouds. Soft mossy lawns
Beneath these canopies extend their swells,
Fragrant with perfumed herbs, and eyed with blooms
Minute yet beautiful. One darkest glen

Sends from its woods of musk-rose, twined with jasmine,
A soul-dissolving odour to invite
To some more lovely mystery. Through the dell,
Silence and Twilight here, twin-sisters, keep
Their noonday watch, and sail among the shades,
Like vaporous shapes half-seen; beyond, a well,
Dark, gleaming, and of most translucent wave,
Images all the woven boughs above,
And each depending leaf, and every speck
Of azure sky, darting between their chasms;
Nor aught else in the liquid mirror laves
Its portraiture, but some inconstant star
Between one foliaged lattice twinkling fair,
Or painted bird, sleeping beneath the moon,
Or gorgeous insect floating motionless,
Unconscious of the day, ere yet his wings
Have spread their glories to the gaze of noon.

Hither the Poet came. His eyes beheld
Their own wan light through the reflected lines
Of his thin hair, distinct in the dark depth
Of that still fountain; as the human heart,
Gazing in dreams over the gloomy grave,
Sees its own treacherous likeness there. He heard
The motion of the leaves, the grass that sprung
Startled and glanced and trembled even to feel
An unaccustomed presence, and the sound
Of the sweet brook that from the secret springs
Of that dark fountain rose. A Spirit seemed
To stand beside him clothed in no bright robes
Of shadowy silver or enshrining light,
Borrowed from aught the visible world affords
Of grace, or majesty, or mystery;
But, undulating woods, and silent well,
And leaping rivulet, and evening gloom
Now deepening the dark shades, for speech assuming,
Held commune with him, as if he and it
Were all that was, only...when his regard
Was raised by intense pensiveness,...two eyes,
Two starry eyes, hung in the gloom of thought,
And seemed with their serene and azure smiles
To beckon him.

Obedient to the light
That shone within his soul, he went, pursuing
The windings of the dell. The rivulet,
Wanton and wild, through many a green ravine

Beneath the forest flowed. Sometimes it fell
Among the moss with hollow harmony
Dark and profound. Now on the polished stones
It danced; like childhood laughing as it went:
Then, through the plain in tranquil wanderings crept,
Reflecting every herb and drooping bud
That overhung its quietness. 'O stream!
Whose source is inaccessibly profound,
Whither do thy mysterious waters tend?
Thou imagest my life. Thy darksome stillness,
Thy dazzling waves, thy loud and hollow gulfs,
Thy searchless fountain, and invisible course
Have each their type in me; and the wide sky,
And measureless ocean may declare as soon
What oozy cavern or what wandering cloud
Contains thy waters, as the universe
Tell where these living thoughts reside, when stretched
Upon thy flowers my bloodless limbs shall waste
I' the passing wind!'

Beside the grassy shore
Of the small stream he went; he did impress
On the green moss his tremulous step, that caught
Strong shuddering from his burning limbs. As one
Roused by some joyous madness from the couch
Of fever, he did move; yet, not like him,
Forgetful of the grave, where, when the flame
Of his frail exultation shall be spent,
He must descend. With rapid steps he went
Beneath the shade of trees, beside the flow
Of the wild babbling rivulet; and now
The forest's solemn canopies were changed
For the uniform and lightsome evening sky.
Grey rocks did peep from the spare moss, and stemmed
The struggling brook; tall spires of windlestrae
Threw their thin shadows down the rugged slope,
And nought but gnarled roots of ancient pines
Branchless and blasted, clenched with grasping roots
The unwilling soil. A gradual change was here,
Yet ghastly. For, as fast years flow away,
The smooth brow gathers, and the hair grows thin
And white, and where irradiate dewy eyes
Had shone, gleam stony orbs: so from his steps
Bright flowers departed, and the beautiful shade
Of the green groves, with all their odorous winds
And musical motions. Calm, he still pursued
The stream, that with a larger volume now

Rolled through the labyrinthine dell; and there
Fretted a path through its descending curves
With its wintry speed. On every side now rose
Rocks, which, in unimaginable forms,
Lifted their black and barren pinnacles
In the light of evening, and its precipice
Obscuring the ravine, disclosed above,
Mid toppling stones, black gulfs and yawning caves,
Whose windings gave ten thousand various tongues
To the loud stream. Lo! where the pass expands
Its stony jaws, the abrupt mountain breaks,
And seems, with its accumulated crags,
To overhang the world: for wide expand
Beneath the wan stars and descending moon
Islanded seas, blue mountains, mighty streams,
Dim tracts and vast, robed in the lustrous gloom
Of leaden-coloured even, and fiery hills
Mingling their flames with twilight, on the verge
Of the remote horizon. The near scene,
In naked and severe simplicity,
Made contrast with the universe. A pine,
Rock-rooted, stretched athwart the vacancy
Its swinging boughs, to each inconstant blast
Yielding one only response, at each pause
In most familiar cadence, with the howl
The thunder and the hiss of homeless streams
Mingling its solemn song, whilst the broad river
Foaming and hurrying o'er its rugged path,
Fell into that immeasurable void
Scattering its waters to the passing winds.

Yet the grey precipice and solemn pine
And torrent were not all; one silent nook
Was there. Even on the edge of that vast mountain,
Upheld by knotty roots and fallen rocks,
It overlooked in its serenity
The dark earth, and the bending vault of stars.
It was a tranquil spot, that seemed to smile
Even in the lap of horror. Ivy clasped
The fissured stones with its entwining arms,
And did embower with leaves for ever green,
And berries dark, the smooth and even space
Of its inviolated floor, and here
The children of the autumnal whirlwind bore,
In wanton sport, those bright leaves, whose decay,
Red, yellow, or ethereally pale,
Rivals the pride of summer. 'Tis the haunt

Of every gentle wind, whose breath can teach
The wilds to love tranquillity. One step,
One human step alone, has ever broken
The stillness of its solitude: one voice
Alone inspired its echoes; even that voice
Which hither came, floating among the winds,
And led the loveliest among human forms
To make their wild haunts the depository
Of all the grace and beauty that endued
Its motions, render up its majesty,
Scatter its music on the unfeeling storm,
And to the damp leaves and blue cavern mould,
Nurses of rainbow flowers and branching moss,
Commit the colours of that varying cheek,
That snowy breast, those dark and drooping eyes.

The dim and horned moon hung low, and poured
A sea of lustre on the horizon's verge
That overflowed its mountains. Yellow mist
Filled the unbounded atmosphere, and drank
Wan moonlight even to fulness; not a star
Shone, not a sound was heard; the very winds,
Danger's grim playmates, on that precipice
Slept, clasped in his embrace. O, storm of death!
Whose sightless speed divides this sullen night:
And thou, colossal Skeleton, that, still
Guiding its irresistible career
In thy devastating omnipotence,
Art king of this frail world, from the red field
Of slaughter, from the reeking hospital,
The patriot's sacred couch, the snowy bed
Of innocence, the scaffold and the throne,
A mighty voice invokes thee. Ruin calls
His brother Death. A rare and regal prey
He hath prepared, prowling around the world;
Glutted with which thou mayst repose, and men
Go to their graves like flowers or creeping worms,
Nor ever more offer at thy dark shrine
The unheeded tribute of a broken heart.

When on the threshold of the green recess
The wanderer's footsteps fell, he knew that death
Was on him. Yet a little, ere it fled,
Did he resign his high and holy soul
To images of the majestic past,
That paused within his passive being now,
Like winds that bear sweet music, when they breathe

Through some dim latticed chamber. He did place
His pale lean hand upon the rugged trunk
Of the old pine. Upon an ivied stone
Reclined his languid head, his limbs did rest,
Diffused and motionless, on the smooth brink
Of that obscurest chasm; and thus he lay,
Surrendering to their final impulses
The hovering powers of life. Hope and despair,
The torturers, slept; no mortal pain or fear
Marred his repose; the influxes of sense,
And his own being unalloyed by pain,
Yet feebler and more feeble, calmly fed
The stream of thought, till he lay breathing there
At peace, and faintly smiling: his last sight
Was the great moon, which o'er the western line
Of the wide world her mighty horn suspended,
With whose dun beams inwoven darkness seemed
To mingle. Now upon the jagged hills
It rests; and still as the divided frame
Of the vast meteor sunk, the Poet's blood,
That ever beat in mystic sympathy
With nature's ebb and flow, grew feebler still:
And when two lessening points of light alone
Gleamed through the darkness, the alternate gasp
Of his faint respiration scarce did stir
The stagnate night: till the minutest ray
Was quenched, the pulse yet lingered in his heart.
It paused, it fluttered. But when heaven remained
Utterly black, the murky shades involved
An image, silent, cold, and motionless,
As their own voiceless earth and vacant air.
Even as a vapour fed with golden beams
That ministered on sunlight, ere the west
Eclipses it, was now that wondrous frame
No sense, no motion, no divinity
A fragile lute, on whose harmonious strings
The breath of heaven did wander, a bright stream
Once fed with many-voiced waves, a dream
Of youth, which night and time have quenched forever,
Still, dark, and dry, and unremembered now.

Oh, for Medea's wondrous alchemy,
Which wheresoe'er it fell made the earth gleam
With bright flowers, and the wintry boughs exhale
From vernal blooms fresh fragrance! O, that God,
Profuse of poisons, would concede the chalice
Which but one living man has drained, who now,

Vessel of deathless wrath, a slave that feels
No proud exemption in the blighting curse
He bears, over the world wanders forever,
Lone as incarnate death! O, that the dream
Of dark magician in his visioned cave,
Raking the cinders of a crucible
For life and power, even when his feeble hand
Shakes in its last decay, were the true law
Of this so lovely world! But thou art fled,
Like some frail exhalation; which the dawn
Robes in its golden beams, ah! thou hast fled!
The brave, the gentle and the beautiful,
The child of grace and genius. Heartless things
Are done and said i' the world, and many worms
And beasts and men live on, and mighty Earth
From sea and mountain, city and wilderness,
In vesper low or joyous orison,
Lifts still its solemn voice: but thou art fled
Thou canst no longer know or love the shapes
Of this phantasmal scene, who have to thee
Been purest ministers, who are, alas!
Now thou art not. Upon those pallid lips
So sweet even in their silence, on those eyes
That image sleep in death, upon that form
Yet safe from the worm's outrage, let no tear
Be shed not even in thought. Nor, when those hues
Are gone, and those divinest lineaments,
Worn by the senseless wind, shall live alone
In the frail pauses of this simple strain,
Let not high verse, mourning the memory
Of that which is no more, or painting's woe
Or sculpture, speak in feeble imagery
Their own cold powers. Art and eloquence,
And all the shows o' the world are frail and vain
To weep a loss that turns their lights to shade.
It is a woe "too deep for tears," when all
Is reft at once, when some surpassing Spirit,
Whose light adorned the world around it, leaves
Those who remain behind, not sobs or groans,
The passionate tumult of a clinging hope;
But pale despair and cold tranquillity,
Nature's vast frame, the web of human things,
Birth and the grave, that are not as they were.

www.ingramcontent.com/pod-product-compliance
Lightning Source LLC
Chambersburg PA
CBHW061249040426
42444CB00010B/2321